PSILOCYBE MUSHROOMS AND THEIR ALLIES

for John Landin —

may this book make the

path to teacanaotl an enjoyable one.

Paul Stamets
October 9th 1978

PAUL STAMETS

PSILOCYBE MUSHROOMS & THEIR ALLIES

HOMESTEAD BOOK COMPANY | SEATTLE

PRODUCED AND EDITED BY BOB HARRIS
DESIGNED BY HOWARD JACOBSEN

*Published by Homestead Book Company,
4009 Stone Way North,
Seattle, Washington 98103.*

*Distributed nationally by And/Or Press,
Box 2246, Berkeley, California 94702.*

*Composition by Community Type &
Design, San Rafael, California; production
by Marilyn Langfeld, Michael Sykes, and
David Lubin.*

*Printed and bound by George Banta
Company, Menasha, Wisconsin.*

*ISBN 0-930180-03-8
LC 77-26546*

*There are certain species of mushrooms in this
book currently restricted by law because of
their chemical content. We in no way
encourage or promote the gathering of species
restricted by law. Our sole aim is to contribute
to the botanical literature.*

CONTENTS

LIST OF ILLUSTRATIONS

Photographs

Diagrams

FOREWORD

THE knowledge of hallucinogenic mushrooms has spanned four major periods of time. The first was the use of these mushrooms by the indigenous tribes of Prehispanic Mexico, whom we have read about in the writings of Sahagún, Motolina, Francisco Hernández, and other Spaniards of the sixteenth century, who mention the *teonanácatl*, the mushroom which makes one intoxicated when it is eaten. The second period, a time of confusion about the real identification of these mushrooms, lasted until the 1950s! The third period consisted of mycological and ethnological expeditions proposing to taxonomically identify the hallucinogenic mushrooms and to become acquainted with the indigenous groups who used them, as well as their chemistry, physiology, and their application in medicine. This period, no doubt the golden age in the knowledge of hallucinogenic mushrooms, is marked by the works of Reko, Schultes, Singer, Wasson, Heim, Smith, Hofmann, and Guzmán, among others. Finally, the present period is characterized by the use of hallucinogenic mushrooms by the young as a recreational drug and by psychologists proposing to study the human mind through the use of these peculiar organisms.

Currently, the production of a great amount of literature on how to collect, identify, cultivate, and ingest these mushrooms is quite notable. Many of these publications are plagued with inaccuracies, principally in the taxonomic aspect, since the group of hallucinogenic mushrooms is very complex and difficult to deal with. The scientific contributions concerning hallucinogenic mushrooms are very few compared to such popular works. Paul Stamets has been preparing this book on the taxonomy of the genus *Psilocybe* for several years with the purpose of elucidating the many problems concerning this genus, which has many species that contain psilocybin as well as many that do not.

Psilocybe Mushrooms and Their Allies fills an important void on how to taxonomically identify the hallucinogenic mushrooms and their allies which grow prolifically in the United States, in which a great deal of interest has developed. Stamets undertakes a major taxonomic revision of all known species in the United States of the genera *Psilocybe, Stropharia, Naematoloma,* and *Panaeolus*, with the purpose of identifying the hallucinogenic mushrooms and separating them from those which are not. The analytical keys he has developed permit the reader to recognize these species with a certain facility not previously possible. Stamets' work is an excellent contribution to the knowledge of not only the hallucinogenic species, but of all the genera mentioned whose species grow in the United States.

Dr. Gastón Guzmán   *ENCB Herbarium*
Mexico City
January 1978

PREFACE

WHEN I first noticed mushrooms, I was overwhelmed by their vast diversity. For years, I viewed mushrooms with mild interest but never focused on them individually. In autumn of one year, my brother and I were hiking in the North Cascades near Darrington, Washington. The trail wound along a steep river canyon leading deep into virgin rain forest. We were in one of those periods of fall so characteristic of the Northwest with the rain falling incessantly for days on end. As we walked along, I had been casually aware of the abundant myco-flora pushing up through the duff of the moss-carpeted forest floor. Pausing at a bend in the trail beneath some towering old-growth cedar, our gaze was imme-diately drawn to a stunning violet mushroom on the upper bank. Upon parting some ferns and investigating further, we were delighted to discover several more pristine specimens. (Later, these keyed out to be *Cortinarius violaceus.*) From that experience on, I have been immersed in the study of mushrooms.

As I sought to know them better, it became apparent there were more species than I could ever hope to recognize in the brevity of a single lifetime. I spent countless hours collecting in the woods and fields, enrolled in mushroom classes, and bought nearly every mushroom book on the market. Yet the more I studied mushrooms, the more I realized how little I had known about them all along. An unending parade of species presented themselves and demanded recognition. Their diversity seemed infinite.

Since I have always had an interest in altered states of consciousness, it was only natural my path should soon lead to the psilocybin-containing mushrooms, par-ticularly of the genera *Psilocybe* and *Panaeolus.* I was increasingly impressed by the similarities among these mushrooms and related genera and species. None of the professed 'field guides' on psilocybian mushrooms acknowledged the importance of studying *Psilocybe* in relation to all fleshy fungi. Rather, they boldly suggested an amateur should go into the field and try to find hallucinogenic mushrooms given only isolated descriptions of a few species. This narrow approach to mushroom identification is dangerously inadequate.

Finding psilocybian species takes time, knowledge, and dedication. In writing this field guide, I felt it essential to emphasize the inherent relationships that hallucinogenic species share with all mushrooms. Surely everyone who has hunted hallucinogenic or edible mushrooms has encountered a vast array of species, many of which resemble the sought-after varieties. To a degree, all these mushrooms are related to one another and often the separation of species becomes a subtle process. Because deadly poisonous species exist, it is vitally important to be equipped with a broad mushroom awareness. This inspired me to construct a genuine field guide to the family of mushrooms containing most of the psilocybian species (the Strophariaceae) by showing the relationships hallucinogenic species have in common with all mushrooms. After becoming familiar with a mushroom's overall nature—its appearances, habits and habitats, and its affinities to closely related species—the task of finding and identifying psilocybian mushrooms is rendered much easier. This field guide represents the culmination of these ideas.

PSILOCYBE MUSHROOMS AND THEIR ALLIES

INTRODUCTION

THROUGH the ages hallucinogenic plants have been employed for religious, medicinal, and hedonistic purposes. Our present day understanding of the historical use of psychotropic mushrooms in other civilizations largely rests on the works of Drs. Blas Pablo Reko, Richard E. Schultes, R. Gordon Wasson, and Roger Heim. They were first to discover and document the utilization of psychotropic mushrooms in shamanic ceremonies of certain Indians of Mexico, particularly in the Sierra Mazateca of Oaxaca. Their research has supported the theory that these modern day mushroom cults are the remnants of an ancient religion practiced by the Aztec and highland Mayan civilizations of the New World. The discovery of mushroom motifs and 'mushroom stones' in excavations of the Indian civilizations strongly suggests the important cultural role these mushrooms had played. The natives revered the mushrooms as a holy sacrament called *teonanácatl,* or 'God's Flesh' in the Aztec language Nahuatl. In the sixteenth century, the expedition of the Spanish conqueror Cortés reported the ritualistic use of *teonanácatl* by the Aztec peoples. However, Catholic missionaries in carrying out their campaign against 'pagan idolatry' soon forced this practice into secrecy, where it has remained hidden until this century.

The overwhelming evidence points to *teonanácatl* as being psilocybin-containing mushroom. The psilocybian species grow across much of North America as well, and are found most profusely on the West Coast, particularly in the Pacific Northwest. Soon after ingesting these mushrooms, a peculiar intoxification is felt. Of course, one's experience depends upon a host of cultural, environmental, and psychological factors as well as the amount and potency of the species eaten. In a similar context, we should view the following description of R. Gordon Wasson's extraordinary vision while under the influence of *Psilocybe caerulescens.*

We were never more wide awake, and the visions came whether our eyes were opened or closed. They emerged from the center of the field of vision, opening as they came, now rushing, now slowly, at the pace our will chose. They were in vivid color, and always harmonious. They began with art motifs, angular such as might decorate carpets of textiles or wall paper of the drawing board of an architect. . . . Later, it was as though the walls of our house had dissolved and my spirit had flown forth, and I was suspended in mid-air viewing landscapes of mountains, with camel caravans advancing slowly across the slopes, the mountains rising tier about tier to the very heavens. . . . It seemed as though I was viewing a world of which I was not a part and with which I could not hope to establish contact. There I was, poised in space, a disembodied eye, invisible, incorporeal, seeing but not seen (R. Gordon Wasson, "Seeking the Magic Mushrooms," *Life,* 13 May 1957, pp. 102, 109).

Such an altered state of consciousness can persist for three to six hours, or even longer, followed by a complete and rapid recovery to ordinary awareness. Often the mycophage reports feeling a sense of ecstatic physical and mental well-being.

In the Pacific Northwest alone, there are an estimated several thousand mushroom species. Most are small and brown, and only a dozen of these contain psilocybin and/or psilocin. By toxic species alone, the psilocybian species are outnumbered at least ten to one. Though fewer species grow in other parts of the country, these basic proportions remain true. Nonetheless, the knowledgeable mushroom hunter can find these psychoactive dark purple brown the black spored mushrooms under the proper environmental conditions and with good field technique. When searching the woods and fields for psilocybian mushrooms, the collector soon encounters a vast array of species similar to the hallucinogenic varieties and sharing common habitats. To know only what a particular *Psilocybe* looks like and yet have no understanding of the many related genera of fungi is foolish and potentially dangerous. Becoming familiar with other groups of mushrooms is prudent, and for good reason.

Some mushrooms which generally resemble *Psilocybe* can be deadly poisonous. Species belonging the the *Galerina autumnalis* and *Galerina marginata* complexes contain the same amatoxins found in the lethal species of *Amanita,* such as *Amanita phalloides* and *Amanita verna,* the 'Destroying Angel'. The general aspect of *Galerina autumnalis* closely parallels that of *Psilocybe,* differing macroscopically only in the overall color of the spores and to a lesser degree in the color of the caps. (*Galerina* spores are rusty brown in deposit while *Psilocybe* spores are purplish brown. Also, the dried color of the caps approximate one another.) *Conocybe filaris,* another rust brown spored mushroom, likewise contains these deadly amatoxins. I commonly find *Psilocybe* growing within inches of *Galerina autumnalis* and *Conocybe filaris!* One dramatic example of this occurrence is illustrated in Fig. 1. Two colonies of mushrooms, one of *G. autumnalis* and the other of *P. stuntzii,* had intersected. In one case the species were growing so close that the stems of the deadly poisonous and hallucinogenic varieties were actually touching. Beware of *Galerina* species and *Conocybe filaris,* as accidental consumption of a sufficient quantity results in horrible, prolonged death. The following is a description of the symptoms resulting from eating *Amanita phalloides*. Similar effects can be expected after eating the above named species of *Galerina* and *Conocybe*.

> First symptoms come late—6–24 hours (average 10–14 hours) after ingestion of the mushrooms. Sharp abdominal pains are followed by violent vomiting and a persistent cholera-like diarrhea (often containing blood and mucus). These symptoms tend to subside and the patient appears to improve. In three to four days the patient's condition begins to worsen with symptoms of liver and kidney failure leading to death in seven to ten days. Autopsy findings are: marked gastro-intestinal edema, hemorrhagic gastro-entiritis, lymphoid tissue and lymph node hyperplasia, fatty degeneration of the heart and liver similar to that seen in carbon tetrachloride poisoning, tubular necrosis of the kidneys, and swollen brain with multiple hemorrhages and degenerative nerve cell damage. Death is primarily from liver and kidney failure. . . . The late onset of symptoms makes early treatment of relatively little help (*Mushroom Poisoning in the Pacific Northwest* [Seattle: Puget Sound Mycological Society, 1972], p. 4).

Other brown and pinkish brown spored genera which should be avoided because of their poisonous properties are *Inocybe*, *Hebeloma*, and *Entoloma*. By taking spore prints and properly using the keys in this book, one precludes the possibility of ingesting these poisonous mushrooms.

1 | Mushrooms: Habits and Habitats

FORTUNATELY, the onset of modern day civilization has not deterred the proliferation of psilocybian mushrooms. Rather, certain psilocybes have profited from man's manipulation of the environment. The relatively sudden arrival of vast, fertile grasslands following the disappearance of lowland forests certainly encouraged the spread of field inhabiting mushrooms across the North American continent. In urban and suburban areas of the Pacific Northwest, the popular practice of spreading wood chips around buildings and lawns has unwittingly provided perfect habitats in which hallucinogenic and poisonous species flourish. With the existence of these new habitats and the importation of exotic plants, non-native species also have been introduced.

Many species in our area were undoubtedly brought from other parts of the world. *Psilocybe semilanceata,* the well-known Liberty Cap, is found in France and throughout much of Europe, while *Psilocybe cyanescens* was first described by Wakefield in England. Both of these species are now established members of the west coast mycoflora and range in distribution from northern California to British Columbia. The presence of *Psilocybe cubensis* in the New World seems to have corresponded with the arrival of Spanish missionaries and the North African cattle they brought with them. Now it is common in Mexico, the Caribbean, and throughout the southeastern United States as far north as Tennessee. There are some unsubstantiated reports of this species growing as far west as California. This is the most commonly cultivated of hallucinogenic mushrooms; it would not be too surprising to find strains adapted to temperate climates appearing in more northern latitudes of this continent.

There are a number of species indigenous to certain geographical localities and not found outside of them. *Psilocybe stuntzii,* both the field and lignicolous varieties, are native to the Pacific Northwest with no reports of this species occurring elsewhere. However, many species may be more widespread than presently believed. As more attention is directed towards the psilocybian species, understanding of them will expand. Amateurs can play an especially important role in contributing to the growing reservoir of knowledge concerning hallucinogenic mushrooms and their allies. Whether psilocybes are actually becoming more common or awareness of them has become so highly specialized, it is evident they are prolific across much of this continent and even the world.

Field Technique

The essence of hunting hallucinogenic mushrooms revolves around developing a very specialized awareness. Since most of the psilocybian mushrooms are small in comparison to the common edible varieties, the technique for finding them is in general much more subtle. I have derived great pleasure in observing mushroom hunting techniques of different individuals. Some older mycophiles I know insist one of the better ways to hunt large edible varieties (such as species of *Agaricus, Boletus, Lepiota*) is to drive down country roads usually at no less than forty mph constantly glancing out the windows. When something resembling a mushroom is spotted, the car screeches to a halt and one person is sent to investigate. Though this technique may work for finding *Psilocybe cubensis,* the renowned Golden Top of the Deep South, it is hardly practical for finding other psilocybian species.

Others I know choose the random fast-walk style of leaning forward at a precarious tilt and walking in a quick gait. They also succeed in finding mushrooms, but one wonders how many species are left trampled and unnoticed in their meandering path. *Psilocybe semilanceata* hunters have a very distinctive method. They are commonly seen stooped way over, sometimes on their hands and knees, carefully searching through the grass before them. During a good fruiting of this prolific northwestern species, it is not unusual to pick several hundred specimens in a few hours. Of course, there is no one technique for finding mushrooms; a keen eye is all that is needed.

What is important in developing good field technique are the ways by which the mushrooms are collected. When picking a mushroom be sure to get the entire fruiting body, especially the base of the stem. I usually take my finger or a knife and carefully dig beneath the entire plant. Then, by gently lifting upwards, the mushroom is picked fully intact. Do not dig up a great deal of the substrate hosting the mushroom mycelium. You can severely damage a colony by removing the rich topsoil so critical to *primordia* formation (see Appendix 1). If you know the species and think you may want to ingest them later on, clean each mushroom as it is picked. This will save you the inconvenience of removing dirt which tends to spread over the collection by the time you return home.

By far the best container in which to carry mushrooms is the wicker basket. Many people have discovered large plastic clothesbaskets are very useful for making large collections. Wrapping individual species in wax paper bags preserves the specimens until you have the opportunity to work on them. Wax paper allows the mushrooms to breathe by slowly releasing water, whereas plastic tends to trap moisture, causing the mushrooms to quickly decompose. The wax paper also acts to some extent as a housing protecting the mushroom specimens from being crushed by the weight of other collections.

Each collection should be labeled and any notable features that might aid in identification recorded (bruising reactions, aspect, habitat, etc.). If you expect to work from fresh collections, and I strongly urge you do, extensive notes may not be necessary. However, when suspecting you have an unusual find, thoroughly describe and photograph the collection. Dry, label, and save your specimens! Amateurs often find previously undescribed or 'new' species. The importance of spore printing all questionable and unfamiliar species cannot be emphasized enough. Though this may seem tedious and a hassle to some, it is absolutely essential for obtaining workable collections and utilizing any systematic approach to mushroom identification. Without good field technique, establishing the identity of unfamiliar species becomes very difficult, if not impossible.

Preservation

For preserving the potency of psilocybian species, freeze-drying is undoubtedly the best method. Though this is the case, freeze-dried mushrooms tend to crumble easily and the process is not readily available to the general public. For all practical purposes, the next best method is to thoroughly dry the specimens and then freeze them sealed in air-tight plastic bags. Drying the mushrooms in a fruit drier works well though the process is somewhat slow, taking a day or two for complete dehydration. Using a baseboard heater and placing the mushrooms so the heat comes up around them is probably one of the better methods; drying the mushrooms takes a matter of a few hours. Any system utilizing the flow of warm air past the specimens works well. Label each collection as to species, date collected, and location, and note any other pertinent data.

All species gradually lose their potency with time, though they may remain active for as long as several years after collecting. To a large degree, it depends on the species, the proportions of psilocybin and psilocin in the original fresh collections, and the way the mushrooms are handled. Of all the psilocybian mushrooms, *Psilocybe semilanceata* appears to degrade most slowly, making it an excellent species to store over long periods of time.

Taking a Spore Print

The mushroom fruiting body continually drops spores from the time the cap expands first exposing the gills. As the plant matures, more and more spores

FIG. 1. Spore print.

are let loose into the atmosphere. The color of the gills often does not reflect spore color, due to the density of spore producing cells (called *basidia;* see Appendix 1) and to a degree by the color of the underlying flesh of the mushroom gill.

Within most genera, the color of a fresh spore deposit is a constant feature. The majority of generic distinctions are at least partially based on the color of the spores. For the amateur, the taking of spore prints is an easy and fairly definitive means for separating groups of mushrooms from one another. *Psilocybe* and *Panaeolus,* genera that include the preponderance of psilocybian species, have spore deposits generally purplish brown to black in color. The previously mentioned genera that contain many toxic species have spore deposits some shade of light brown, except for *Amanita* which is whitish. *Conocybe* and *Galerina* are rusty brown, *Entoloma* is salmon-pinkish brown, *Hebeloma* and *Inocybe* are yellowish brown to clay brown to dull brown. Though these are some of the more prominent hazardous brown spored genera, keep in mind there are an abundance of toxic species in other genera as well. (Consult texts in the Annotated Bibliography of General Mushroom Field Guides.)

The technique for taking a spore print is very simple. It is best to get a spore deposit soon after the mushroom has been picked. As the mushroom dries it becomes more difficult to obtain a print. By placing the mushroom in a wax paper bag (not plastic—the mushrooms have to breathe), a spore print can usually be obtained within an hour or two after picking at most. From each collection choose several fresh but fairly mature specimens. Separate the cap from the stem of each carpophore with a knife and place the cap, gills down, on a piece of white paper or on a Petri dish. If the spore print is not being taken in the field and you have returned home after hunting, it is best to place a glass or cup over each cap to lessen the rate of dehydration and disturbance from air currents. It is also a good idea to put a few drops of water inside the glass for mushrooms likely to be difficult in obtaining a spore deposit. In the matter of a few hours, the spores will deposit on the paper according to the radiating symmetry of the gills, thus indicating the spore color in mass. If you suspect the spores will be white, take the print on dark paper. Upon identifying the mushroom collection, label the print and save. If you desire to cultivate the species printed, these spores can be used to establish cultures.

The Bluing Reaction

A feature common to many of the psilocybian mushrooms is the 'bluing reaction'. Many *Psilocybe* and *Panaeolus* species will turn bluish or bluish green when bruised. This happens either normally in response to growing conditions or in handling as they are picked. The bluing reaction is of great interest to chemists and pharmacologists. Even mushroom taxonomists consider it a valuable character for delineating groups of species. Apparently, the blue pigmentation is a result of psilocin (dephosphorylated psilocybin) degradation to presently unknown compounds by enzymes within the mushroom cells. What this means is that when a *Psilocybe* or *Panaeolus* bruises bluish, it is a very good indication that psilocybin and/or psilocin is present. Naturally, since this is a degradation process, the more the mushrooms are bruised, the less potent they become.

However, this feature has limited importance from the taxonomist's point of view. Many active *Psilocybe* and *Panaeolus* species will not blue no matter how you abuse them, and there are several poisonous and suspect species outside these two genera which exhibit 'bluing' though no psilocybin or psilocin is present. For instance, *Hygrophorus conicus* (Fr.) Fr. and allies turn brilliantly bluish black when disturbed, and they are highly suspect, though the chemistry is still unknown. *Inocybe calminstrata* (Fr.) Quel. has a stem that is often blue at the base, and this species—as well as all species within the genus *Inocybe*—should be avoided. I have also collected mushrooms belonging to the deadly genus *Galerina* whose stems have turned blackish blue from the base upwards. This bluish black coloration, especially at the stem base, is not an uncommon feature in the mushroom world.

Within the dark purplish brown to black spored genera, the bluing reaction can be an excellent parameter for narrowing the field of possible mushroom species to the psilocybian fungi. It is not very useful for determining the identity of individual species, nor is it useful for identifying all of the active psilocybes and panaeoli. As with any indicator, the bluing phenomenon has its place and its limitations.

Chemical Myths

Metol is practically useless for establishing the presence of psilocybin or psilocin. It gives a 'positive' reaction with a host of distantly related species. In fact, most of the mushrooms I have immersed in a Metol solution have turned the liquid bluish or purplish, as undoubtedly thousands of bewildered mushroom hunters have discovered on their own.

In a recent book on cultivation (F.C. Ghouled and Richard Meredith, *Psilocybin Cultivation* [Chapel Hill: Design Books, 1976]), the authors boldly imply that Melzer's iodine will help field hunters identify psilocybin containing mushrooms. They urge you to be careful by crushing a specimen and placing it in the Melzer's solution. If the liquid (and flesh) turn bluish, then psilocybin is present. This is very deceiving; though a bluing reaction may be noted, it is not a definitive indication of the presence of psilocybin. The flesh of species of *Chroogomphus* turns bluish in this solution; even spores of *Amanita virosa*, the Destroying Angel, exhibit the amyloid blue reaction. Like Metol, it is non-specific for determining psilocybin content, though it can be useful for separating species within a genus.

2 | Taxonomy

A TRAIT intrinsic to human nature is the desire to place labels on objects. Only after man has assigned a name to something can it be used economically in a language. Without precise labels, we would be left in the perplexing position of gesturing and rambling inordinately in the attempt to communicate the appearance of some particular form. By labeling objects, we are incorporating them into a framework of thinking and by applying a methodical system of classification to a set of these objects, we are implementing a scheme of *taxonomy.*

Our concern is with the classification or taxonomy of mushrooms, especially the psilocybian species and their allies. In the centuries that mycology has existed as a science, fungal taxonomy has always been in a state of continual change and evolution. New species concepts and definitions are forever being formulated— and no wonder, considering that known mushroom species number into the many thousands and that to some degree all these species are interrelated. At what point, one may ask, should two mushroom forms be called separate species, and when do thy become synonomous? This becomes especially difficult to answer with the closest of related species. A standard rule for mycologists is that two mushrooms are of the same species if their spores are compatible.

Though these may seem like academic questions, they are relevant to understanding the basis of our taxonomic system. (By the way, I am not implying that one has to mate spore types to distinguish species, or that only mycologists can identify mushrooms.) The important thing is for laypeople to realize the limitations and advantages of placing an artificial system of classification upon a naturally occuring set of plants. With both amateurs and mycologists, developing skills in identification becomes a matter of learning to recognize significant morphological differences between species. In doing this, we are essentially becoming taxonomists.

Our taxonomic system is fundamentally based on the binomial concept of genus and species. From here, a species can be interpreted from broader or more specific modes of classification. *Psilocybe baeocystis* is listed below to illustrate its placement in the overall taxonomy.

Kingdom	Plantae	The plant kingdom
Phylum	Eumycota	The true fungi
Class	Basidiomycetes	Fungi which produce spores by basidia
Order	Agaricales	The gilled fungi
Family	Strophariaceae	A dark spored family
Genus	*Psilocybe*	(See Chapter 3)
Section	*Caerulescentes*	The bluing species
Stirps	*Cyanescens*	Large spored, non-annulate, non-mycenoid species
Species	*baeocystis*	

The majority of psilocybian species can be found in the families Strophariacae and Coprinaceae, and their spore deposits range from purplish gray to purplish brown to black. In the genus *Conocybe* (of the family Bolbitiaceae) the spores are rust brown in deposit and there are two infrequently encountered species which possess psilocybin and/or psilocin. However, the presence of *Conocybe filaris* in this genus, a species known to contain deadly amatoxins, makes me very reluctant to recommend any experimentation with the conocybes.

The majority of hallucinogenic species of the Coprinaceae family are in the genus *Panaeolus* (see Chapter 3). *Psathyrella* and *Coprinus* along with *Panaeolus* constitute the Coprinaceae. *Panaeolus* can be readily distinguished from other genera of this family by the 'spotted' or mottled appearance of the mature gills from uneven ripening of the spores, and by the fact that most species grow in dung, straw, or grassy areas. *Psathyrella* is somewhat similar, but the gills do not become mottled and their spores fade or discolor in concentrated sulphuric acid. *Coprinus* is very distinct due to the nature of its gills (and the cap) which upon maturity 'melt' or deliquesce into a blackish liquid. What distinguishes this family from the Strophariaceae family is that members of the Coprinaceae have cap cuticles (the surface layer of cells on the caps) composed of rounded, inflated cells, while the latter family has a cuticle made up of long interwoven cells.

The family Strophariaceae includes the genera *Naematoloma, Psilocybe,* and *Stropharia*. The majority of psilocybian species are found in the genus *Psilocybe*. Often *Psilocybe* species cannot be separated wholly from other species of this family using only macroscopic features as there is considerable intergradation of appearances among all three genera. The natural affinities between *Naematoloma, Psilocybe,* and *Stropharia* are evident to anyone who has picked these mushrooms. Therefore, it is more reasonable to view these three genera as one larger entity, a family, than trying to make cut-and-dried distinctions among them (see Chapter 3). This becomes an especially practical approach for amateurs who are not accustomed to separating species microscopically. Dr. Alexander Smith, a noted mycologist, points out that basic difficulties in attempting the clearly distinguish among members of this family in his *Field Guide to Western Mushrooms* (Ann Arbor: Univ. of Michigan Press, 1975, p. 215) by stating, "As the French mycologist L. Quélet realized years ago, the three genera *Psilocybe, Stropharia,* and *Naematoloma* (as *Hypholoma*) in reality constitute a single genus."

Dilemmas in Modern Taxonomy

I have followed the least complicated course in introducing the amateur to the taxonomy of psilocybian mushrooms and their allies. By doing so, the novice has been spared the difficult task of sorting out the perplexing problems inherent in mushroom taxonomy. Specifically how a group of fungi should be classified becomes a matter of mycological interpretation. The debates often become academic with one professional opinion in opposition to another.

Usually these differences in interpretation reflect two dissimilar schools of thought—that of the 'splitters' and the 'lumpers'. The splitters are mycologists who have acquired a reputation for categorizing and delineating species on the most minute details. They interpret mushrooms from a strict taxonomic point of view and are inclined to divide families, genera, and species into more families, genera, and species. In the attempt to match our system of classification as precisely as possible to the world of mushrooms, the taxonomy becomes extremely specialized and complicated.

On the other hand, lumpers are typically mycologists who classify mushrooms with ample license for species variation and intergradation. Rather than establishing a new species or creating a new taxonomic mode based on subtle differences, lumpers tend to interpret species more generally and cautiously. They are more conservative in their approach to identification and with the placement of species in the overall taxonomy.

Both approaches have their merits and disadvantages. My own inclinations lean toward the lumpers, for practical reasons. I have a high regard for species variation and a natural suspicion of catch-all taxons, especially when dealing with genera of the Strophariaceae. The splitter approach is useful to a degree, but when a taxonomy becomes so burdened with overspecialization it flounders in its own intricacies, the system ceases to be effective. A problem with extremely specialized taxonomies is that the knowledge gained frequently gets caught in a labyrinth of 'ifs, ands, or buts' as to be hardly decipherable. Taking into account the nature of the subject matter, one can understand the difficult position of the mushroom taxonomist.

Keeping this in mind, I would like to add a few notes on the affinities the family Strophariaceae have with other families. Because this book has been constructed to be a practical, efficient field guide, I have followed a certain taxonomic interpretation by defining the Strophariaceae as a family with only three members (*Naematoloma, Psilocybe,* and *Stropharia*). There are some mycologists who believe the genus *Panaeolus* should be included within this family as well. Others have an even more inflated concept of the Strophariaceae that includes the genus *Pholiota* (which some mycologists had previously placed in the Cortinariaceae family). *Pholiota* can be distinguished from genera of the Strophariaceae mostly on color of the spore deposits. *Pholiota* spores are typically dark brown to gray brown or rust brown, while the psilocybian species and their allies have spores more purplish brown to black in color. *Pholiota* most closely resembles *Stropharia* and *Naematoloma* in appearance and their presence can cause some confusion in identification if spore prints are not taken.

Essential Terminology

Before a mushroom enthusiast can effectively use this book and its keys, a certain understanding of terminology has to be achieved. I do not go deeply into the sea of expressions mycologists often employ, but many terms cannot be substituted clearly or economically by common words without sacrificing precise shades of meaning. The language utilized here is not difficult to master. To make the transition easier, some of the more frequently encountered terms are listed below. I recommend spending some time familiarizing yourself with them and the different kinds of cap shapes, gill attachments, and other general features illustrated in the diagrams in Chapter 3. With this and the thorough glossary at the end of the book, you should be prepared fully to use the information presented here to its greatest potential.

annulus (membranous) The tissue remnants of the partial veil adhering to the stem to form a collar or membranous ring.

annular zone A band of fibrils around the stem, usually becoming darkened by spores. The annular zone is derived from the partial veil whether it be membranous or cortinate.

appendiculate Hanging or decorated with veil remnants (along the cap margin).

cortina (*adjective:* **cortinate**) A fine web-like veil extending from the cap margin to the stem in young specimens of certain species. Soon disappearing or leaving trace remnants on the stem or cap margin.

FIG. 2. Separable pellicle on *Psilocybe semilanceata.*

evanescent   Fragile, non-permanent, soon vanishing.

fibrils (*adjective:* **fibrillose**)   Fine delicate 'hairs'.

fruiting body   The actual mushroom form or structure, the fruit of the mushroom plant.

membranous   Used in describing a homo-, geneous sheath-like or skin-like tissue characteristic of a type of partial veil.

mycelium   The network of fungi cells which may or may not amass to form the mushroom fruiting body.

partial veil   the inner veil of tissue extending from the cap margin to the stem and at first covering the gills in young fruiting bodies of some species.

pellicle   A 'skin' or upper surface layer of cells on the cap surface which can undergo gelatinization, making the cap viscid to the touch. Often it can be peeled away from the cap.

rhizomorphs   Cord-like strands of twisted mycelia present about the stem in some mushrooms.

striate   Having radial lines or furrows.

translucent-striate   Appearing striate from the translucent quality of the cap through which the gills show.

viscid   Slippery, slimy, or sticky to the touch when wet. In partially dried specimens, it is difficult to tell if the caps were once viscid or not. One field test involves touching the the cap against one's upper lip, and if it sticks, then this is a good indication the cap was originally viscid when wet.

COLOR PLATES

FIG. 3. *Conocybe filaris* complex. Species of this complex can possess dangerously high levels of the deadly toxins also found in *Galerina* and *Amanita*.

FIG. 4. *Conocybe cyanopus* (*sensu* Kühner). A small hallucinogenic mushroom growing in low damp grassy habitats. The base of the stem bruises bluish.

FIG. 5. *Galerina autumnalis* complex. These species can be deadly poisonous and are often encountered when looking for psilocybes.

FIG. 6. *Galerina autumnalis–Psilocybe stuntzii*. Two species, one deadly poisonous and the other hallucinogenic, are growing so closely they appear clustered. They can be definitively separated from one another by spore color, and to a lesser degree by the color of the caps.

FIG. 7. *Naematoloma aurantiaca*. Currently, this species is known only from California though it may be more widely distributed than presently believed. Edibility uncertain.

FIG. 8. *Naematoloma capnoides,* the Smoky Gilled Woodlover, is an edible species and of fairly good flavor.

FIG. 9. *Naematoloma dispersum* can look very similar to *Psilocybe pelliculosa.* Edibility not known.

FIG. 10. *Naematoloma fasciculare,* the Green Gilled Woodlover, is a close relative of *Naematoloma capnoides.* However, it is very bitter and gastro-intestinally poisonous.

FIGS. 11, 12. *Psilocybe baeocystis* is commonly found near *Psilocybe stuntzii* and *Galerina autumnalis.* The undulating margin, best seen in young specimens, is very characteristic of this species. In the fresh state, it is strongly hallucinogenic.

FIG. 13. *Psilocybe caerulescens-zapotecorum* complex (right). *Psilocybe caerulescens,* known as the Landslide Mushroom in Mexico, was first described by Murrill from Alabama. It grows on recent landslides and in sugar cane mulch. Hallucinogenic.

FIG. 14. *Psilocybe coprophila* complex. A group of closely related species center around this mushroom. They are called the dung loving psilocybes and some collections are weakly hallucinogenic.

FIGS. 15, 16. *Psilocybe cubensis* group, the Golden Top or San Isidro (Saint of the Fields), grows across much of the southeastern United States and in subtropical or tropical climes across the world.

FIG. 17. *Psilocybe cubensis* (left) fruiting in grain-filled jar.

FIG. 18. *Psilocybe cyanescens* grows in decayed wood debris, especially heavily mulched areas. First collected in England by Wakefield, it is known to grow only in the western coastal regions of this continent. Strongly hallucinogenic.

FIG. 19. *Psilocybe merdaria* complex. Several species center around this mushroom. The annular zone on the stem is very typical of this species. Some collections are weakly hallucinogenic.

Fig. 20. *Psilocybe montana* is prolific in damp mossy areas during the spring. This mushroom was originally designated the type species upon which the genus is based. Edibility not known.

Fig. 21. *Psilocybe pelliculosa* is a woodland species appearing during the late fall in the northwest. In some collections, the stem will bruise bluish at the base. *Psilocybe silvatica* is nearly identical in appearance to this species. Both are hallucinogenic, though not strongly so.

FIGS. 22, 23. *Psilocybe semilanceata,* the Liberty Cap (above and following page), is perhaps the easiest of northwestern psilocybes to recognize. It grows in grassy areas, most abundantly during the fall and to a lesser degree during the spring.

FIG. 24. *Psilocybe sp.* resembles *Psilocybe cubensis* but has distinctly smaller spores. This species was found in the San Francisco Bay several years ago. Bruising bluish green where touched and apparently hallucinogenic. (Photograph is of cultivated mushroom.)

FIG. 25. *Psilocybe squamosa*, formerly a *Stropharia*, is distinguished by the scales initially adorning the cap and stem. Suspected of being poisonous.

FIG. 26. *Psilocybe strictipes* is very similar to *Psilocybe baeocystis*, differing in certain microscopic features and in the cap-width/stem-length ratio. Hallucinogenic.

FIGS. 27, 28, 29. *Psilocybe stuntzii* group shows a great diversity of forms. It is the only hallucinogenic *Psilocybe* in the northwest to have a distinct annulus.

FIG. 30. *Psilocybe umbonatescens* is a yellowish dung-inhabiting species with a pronounced umbo on its cap. It is fairly rare and not known to be hallucinogenic or poisonous.

FIG. 31. *Stropharia aeruginosa* is a bright bluish to greenish species and sometimes can be fairly large. Historically, this mushroom has been labeled poisonous, though there is limited evidence suggesting it may be psilocybian.

FIG. 32. *Stropharia albocyanea* is closely related to *Stropharia aeruginosa*. Some authors dispute whether it is a valid species or just a form of *aeruginosa*. It is streaked bluish, especially when young. Edibility not known.

FIG. 33. *Stropharia ambigua* (left) is very common in the northwest in the fall and spring. The veil remnants adhering to the cap margin is very distinctive of this species. It is not a good edible.

FIG. 34. *Stropharia coronilla* is a widely distributed grassland species. It is suspected of being poisonous.

FIG. 35. *Stropharia hornemannii* is very common during the fall in the western United States. The cap is usually very viscid when moist and the stem can be very scaly below a well-formed annulus.

FIG. 36. *Stropharia rugoso-annulata,* the wine red *Stropharia,* is known by its large size, the deep reddish color of the young mushroom caps, and the annulus on the stem. It grows mostly in cultivated grounds.

FIGS. 37, 38. *Stropharia semiglobata* thrives in dung or in well-manured grounds. Initially, the stem is covered by a glutinous sheath, making it difficult to grasp. Edible, but of poor quality.

FIG. 39. *Stropharia stercoraria,* another dung-loving mushroom, is very close to *Stropharia semiglobata.* The distinguishing features are largely microscopic. Edibility not known.

FIG. 40. *Panaeolus acuminatus* grows in grassy areas, in dung, and occasionally along the borders of woods. The cap is conic at first, and may expand to nearly plane when fully mature. Not hallucinogenic, not poisonous.

FIGS. 41, 42. *Panaeolus campanulatus-sphinctrinus* complex is represented here by two forms, one grayish and the other brownish. The complex is easy to recognize but the taxonomy is very confused. I have eaten species of this group with no effect. Edible, but of poor quality.

FIG. 43. *Panaeolus castaneifolius* (right) is very close to *Panaeolus foenisecii* in appearance, but has a violet-black spore deposit. Weakly hallucinogenic, if at all.

Fig. 44. *Panaeolus cyanescens,* the Bluing Panaeolus, appears here in pristine condition. *Panaeolus tropicalis* is very similar. Both grow in subtropical regions, such as the southeastern United States, Mexico, and Hawaii. Strongly hallucinogenic.

Fig. 45. *Panaeolus fimicola* complex. Some collections contain psilocybin and psilocin.

FIG. 46. *Panaeolus foenisecii* is a frequently encountered grassland species. It has a dark brownish spore deposit. Some collections have shown low levels of psilocybin to be present.

FIG. 47. *Panaeolus phalaenarum* can be quite large and is somewhat similar to *Panaeolus semiovatus*. According to some authors, it is edible and of good quality.

Fig. 48. *Panaeolus retirugis* prefers decomposed straw piles. Some collections may be hallucinogenic.

FIG. 49. *Panaeolus semiovatus* is the only *Panaeolus* with an annulus on the stem. It is infrequently psilocybian, if at all.

FIG. 50. *Panaeolus subbalteatus* is widely distributed across the continent preferring horse manure and straw habitats. The stem base often bruises bluish green. Hallucinogenic. (Photograph is of cultivated mushrooms.)

3 | The Keys

WHEN identifying mushrooms, mycologists and amateurs commonly use taxonomic keys. In the following pages, there is a collection of keys carefully prepared and tested extensively in the field. The keys function through a process of eliminations. For the most part, they are two-step (*dichotomous*) keys that pair distinguishing characteristics to arrive at species identification. By repeatedly selecting the key leads best fitting the appearance of the unknown mushroom, one is soon led to the species identity. Since the keys use macroscopic (visible) mushroom features, it is necessary for the reader to understand basic mushroom morphology. Most of the essential features are illustrated in Diagrams A, B, and C, while the rest are described in the glossary at the book's end.

In Chapter 2, I explained the value of viewing psilocybian species in the perspective of a family of related mushrooms. By taking spore prints and determining the spore color in mass to be purplish brown to black, and by checking Diagram D and the Generic Key to the Dark Brown to Black Spored Agarics, a person can key out a mushroom collection very closely to genus. Since members of the family Strophariaceae often cross (visual) generic definitions, it is only necessary for a mushroom collection to key out to a genus within this family. Then by turning to the Key to the Strophariaceae, the mushroom can be keyed to species. If, when using the generic keys you are led to *Panaeolus*, consult the key for that genus.

Since this may sound complicated let's use an example. Early one morning we set out hunting mushrooms in western Oregon. In a rich grassy field, we found an interesting but unknown colony of mushrooms. For the time being, they are labeled Mushroom Collection X. Upon carefully examining the find, we note the gills are distinctly attached to the stem in an adnate to sinuate fashion and the straw yellow cap is broadly convex to nearly plane at maturity. Our measurements show the cap to be in the 2–5 cm range and the stem to be no longer than 5 or 6 cm in length and 3–5 mm in thickness. There is a slightly striated membranous annulus on the stem (implying a membranous partial veil) that seems to be very persistent, as we can see it or remnants of it on all of the specimens collected. We also learn that the spore color is dark purplish brown from the deposit on the underside of the annulus and from the spore prints that were taken.

With this information, Mushroom Collection X can be keyed out at least to genus, and in this example, to species. Turning to the pictorial key we see the mushrooms in question most closely resemble species of the genus *Stropharia.* We then go on to the Generic Key to the Dark Brown to Black Spored Agarics and are faced with a choice in key lead **1a.** Do the gills (and cap) deliquesce (melt) or become paper thin with age? Surely this would have been noticed if it was the case with our species. Since that was not observed we go to lead **1b** which then directs us to **2.** Is the partial veil membranous (sometimes floccose), usually leaving a membranous annulus? Or is the partial veil not membranous and no membranous annulus present? The former applies, so following **2a** we are told to go on to **3.** This key lead asks whether the gills are attached or free from the stem, and whether the spore color is chocolate brown or not. Our observations were that it was attached to the stem in an adnate to sinuate fashion and the spore color is not chocolate brown, so we go on to **4.** In **4** we are asked whether the spore deposit is black, purplish brown, or near cinnamon brown to earth brown in color. It is definitely dark purplish brown, and we find our collection keys out to *Stropharia.*

The notes following the key remind us this genus belongs to the family Strophariaceae, and we should turn to the key to that family. By continuing through the family key with the above information, we are soon led to the species identification, that Mushroom Collection X is actually *Stropharia coronilla.* The species description for *Stropharia coronilla* in Chapter 4 tells us that it is neither hallucinogenic nor considered edible, but *it is suspected of being poisonous!* (Many species in *Stropharia* are suspect and little documentation of their toxicity exist.)

If in the above example, we originally found a collection of *Psilocybe* with a distinct annulus, the generic keys would have led us to the genus *Stropharia,* but by going through the family keys, we would have soon been re-routed to the correct genus of this species. Other *Psilocybe* species and some *Stropharia* will key out under *Naematoloma,* while some *Naematoloma* species will key out under *Psilocybe* and *Stropharia.* As these examples show, it is more useful and accurate to have keys to the family Strophariaceae then individual keys to each genus.

Always go through the keys twice to make sure you have not made a mistake. Then find the description of the species in Chapter 4 and read it carefully. Compare the photograph with your collection and note in the descriptions under Comments that similarly appearing and closely related species are suggested as alternative possibilities.

The keys have undergone numerous evolutions to reach their present state, having taken two years of intense study to construct. Try to use them while your collections are still fresh; otherwise take extensive notes on every aspect of the mushroom specimens.

Since the keys are primarily based on macroscopic features for use in the field by the amateur, they have certain limitations from the mycologist's point of view, where light microscopes are considered invaluable for laboratory identification. To minimize the limitations of macroscopic identification, I emphasize keying out species more than once when exhibiting significantly variable characteristics. Microscopic features have also been included in many cases, but only to reinforce macroscopic key leads. A section on basic light microscopy appears in Appendix 2 for those having access to microscopes.

The genus *Panaeolus* and the family Strophariaceae are subject to varying interpretations and difficult taxonomic problems remain unresolved. However, if you are patient and follow the keys carefully, they will lead you to the identification of the unfamiliar mushrooms at hand.

Species Covered in This Book

RUST BROWN SPORED AGARICS

CONOCYBE
cyanopus
filaris
smithii

GALERINA
autumnalis
marginata

PURPLISH BROWN TO BLACK SPORED AGARICS

» The Family Strophariaceae

NAEMATOLOMA
aurantiaca
capnoides
dispersum var. *typica*
dispersum var. *idahoense*
elongatum
ericaeum
fasciculare
olivaceotinctum
polytrichi
popperianum
squalidellum
sublateritium
subochraceum
udum

PSILOCYBE
angustispora
baeocystis
caerulescens
caerulipes
californica
coprophila
corneipes
cubensis
cyanescens
merdaria
montana
pelliculosa
quebecensis
semilanceata
silvatica
sp.

strictipes
stuntzii
  (field variety)
stuntzii (lignicolous
  variety)
subviscida
thrausta
umbonatescens
washingtonensis

STROPHARIA
aeruginosa
albocyanea
albonitens
ambigua
bilamellata
coronilla
hardii
hornemannii
kauffmanii
magnivelaris
melanosperma
rugoso-annulata
semiglobata
semigloboides
siccipes
stercoraria

» The Family Coprinaceae

PANAEOLUS
acuminatus
campanulatus
castaneifolius
cyanescens
fimicola
foenisecii
fontinalis
fraxinophilus
papilionaceus

phalaenarum
retirugis
rickenii
semiovatus
sp.
sphinctrinus
subbalteatus
tropicalis

Coprinus and *Psathyrella* species are not listed.

DIAGRAM A

Cap Shapes

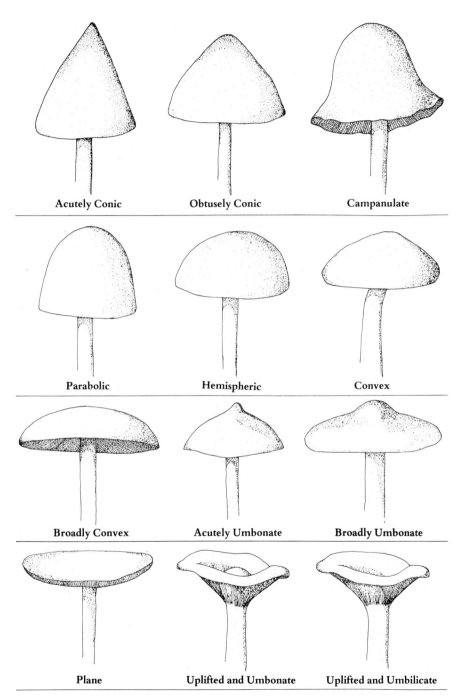

| Acutely Conic | Obtusely Conic | Campanulate |

| Parabolic | Hemispheric | Convex |

| Broadly Convex | Acutely Umbonate | Broadly Umbonate |

| Plane | Uplifted and Umbonate | Uplifted and Umbilicate |

GILL ATTACHMENT

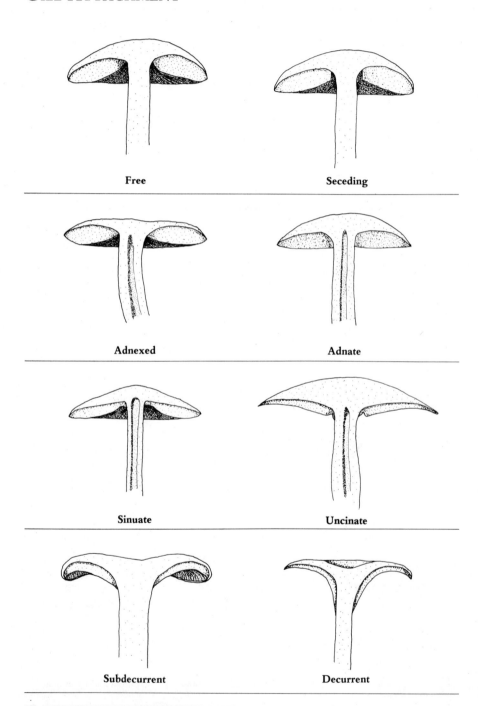

Free

Seceding

Adnexed

Adnate

Sinuate

Uncinate

Subdecurrent

Decurrent

DIAGRAM C

GENERAL MORPHOLOGY

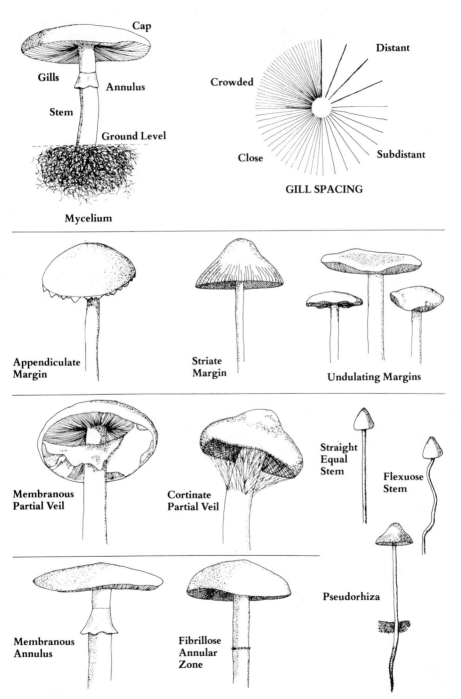

Cap

Gills

Annulus

Stem

Ground Level

Mycelium

Crowded

Distant

Close

Subdistant

GILL SPACING

Appendiculate Margin

Striate Margin

Undulating Margins

Membranous Partial Veil

Cortinate Partial Veil

Straight Equal Stem

Flexuose Stem

Membranous Annulus

Fibrillose Annular Zone

Pseudorhiza

Simplified Picture Key *to 55 Genera of Gilled Mushrooms*

SPORE COLOR GROUP	**I. WHITE TO YELLOW**

FREE GILLS; cap and stem easily removed

Amanitaceae	**Lepiotaceae**
 *Amanita:* Caps warty and/or striate along margin. Stems with or without ring; remnants of volva at base. Habitat on ground.	*Lepiota:* Caps ± scaly (1 species smooth), not viscid when moist. Stems with ring, sometimes disappearing.

SLIM STEMS; texture different from cap

Tricholomaceae

 *Mycena:* Mushrooms small. Caps conic or campanulate, margin straight when young. Stems fragile, often hollow. Habit and habitat usually clustered on wood or ground.

 Xeromphalina: Caps small, umbilicate, flesh thin, yellowish or orangish in color. Stems brown, horny, with orange hairs at base. Habitat on wood. *Omphalina:* Caps similar to above. Gills ± thick and distant. (Colors dull; gills thin, close—small *Clitocybe,* see below.)

 Mature caps flat to umbonate, margin incurved or inrolled when young. Gills variably attached, never decurrent. *Collybia:* Caps soft, fleshy. Stems brittle to fibrous or fleshy. *Marasmius:* Caps pliable or leathery. Stems leathery to horny.

 Gills adnate to decurrent. Stems with a ± distinct ring. *Armillaria:* Caps 2–6 inches. Often clustered on wood. *Cystoderma:* Caps 1–2 inches, grainy. Ring flaring or fragile.

Caps attached to wood by eccentric, absent, or rarely central stems. *Pleurotus:* Caps fleshy. Habit clustered. *Lentinus* and *Lentinellus:* Caps tough. Gills with sawtooth edges. *Panus* and *Panellus:* Caps tough, leathery, revivable. Gills with smooth edges.

 *Phyllotopsis:* Caps attached at their sides or on their tops to wood. Spores salmon buff.

GILLS ATTACHED; cap and stem of similar texture

Hygrophoraceae

 *Hygrophorus:* Caps variably shaped, often glutinous. Gills variable, often decurrent, distant, waxy, wedge-shaped in cross-section. Habitat on ground.

Caps ± convex, umbonate. Stem stiff and fibrous. *Melanoleuca:* Gills close, dry, thin; white to buff. Stems striate, straight. *Laccaria:* Gills distant, waxy, thick; rosy or lilac. Stems twisted, fibrous.

Lyophyllum: Caps usually somber-colored, variably sized and shaped. Gills bruising gray, brown, or black. Stems often water-soaked. (Genus defined chemically: gills go blue with PDAB; basidia have carminophilus granules.)

Russulaceae

 Caps depressed in center. Stems brittle like chalk. *Lactarius:* Gills exuding 'milk' when cut. *Russula:* Gills dry when cut, all gills reach stem.

 Caps often funnel-shaped. Gills ± decurrent. *Clitocybe:* Gills thin and narrow. *Leucopaxillus:* Caps dry, unpolished. Gills and stems dry, chalky. Stem base with much moldy white mycelium.

 Cap surface very variable. Gills sinuate. Stems stout, fleshy. *Tricholoma:* On ground. *Tricholomopsis:* On wood.

SPORE COLOR GROUP	II. PINK TO SALMON	III. YELLOW-BROWN TO RUSTY-BROWN

FREE GILLS; cap and stem easily removed

Volvariaceae

Volvariella: Gills deep salmon colored in age. Stem base with sac-like volva. Habitat varied.

Pluteus (spore color II): Spores salmon. Gills finally deep salmon. Habitat mostly on wood or sawdust.

Bolbitiaceae

Bolbitius: Caps viscid when moist, striate, soft, and egg-yellow. Stems slender, fragile. Often clustered on dung or in grass.

SLIM STEMS; texture different from cap

Rhodophyllaceae

Nolanea: Like *Mycena;* caps often striate when wet. Stems never bluish. *Leptonia:* Caps convex in age, margin incurved when young. Stems slender, polished, often bluish. *Eccilia:* Caps umbilicate, dull. Gills decurrent. Stems soon hollow.

Cortinariaceae

Caps striate, hygrophanous. Stem fibrillose with or without annular zone of fibrils. *Galerina:* Caps thin, convex to umbonate. Gills adnate to sinuate. Stems usually darkened at base. Usually clustered. *Tubaria:* Caps soon plane, ± umbilicate, ± cinnamon. Gills decurrent. Spores pale.

Conocybe: Caps smooth, dull, conic. Stems hollow, fragile. Habitat with grass, on dung..

GILLS ATTACHED; cap and stem of similar texture.

Entoloma: Gills sinuate. Spore deposit and mature gills salmon colored.

Crepidotus: Caps small, attached on one side or on their tops. Usually shelf-like on wood.

Membranous ring may disappear. Habitat on ground. *Agrocybe:* Spores cigar brown.

Rozites: Spores pale brown.

Clitopilus: Caps like kidskin, whitish. Gills decurrent, gray-pink when old. Odor mealy.

Caps and stems fibrillose-scaly. Gill attachment variable. Stems ± rings. Most species tufted on wood. *Pholiota:* Caps may be viscid. Spores brown. *Gymnopilus:* Caps not viscid. Spores rusty orange.

Gills adnate to sinuate, dull brown. Spores dull brown. *Hebeloma:* Caps smooth, silky to viscid. Stems often pallid. *Inocybe:* Caps small, brown, and thready or scaly, not viscid.

Tricholomataceae (cont.)

Lepista: Cap colors lilac, whitish, or buff. Gills sinuate to decurrent. Spore deposit pinkish to buff.

Cortinarius: Caps dry or slimy. Gills rust-brown when old. Stems often bulbous. Partial veil cortinate. Habitat on humus in woods.

Paxillaceae

Paxillus: Cap margin inrolled when young. Gills easily rubbed off in large portions, pore-like near stem. Stems central, off-centered, or lacking. Habitat on wood or ground.

SPORE COLOR GROUP	IV. PURPLE-BROWN TO CHOCOLATE-BROWN	V. BLACKISH
FREE GILLS; cap and stem easily removed	**Agaricaceae** *Agaricus:* Cap dry, smooth or ± scaly. Gills free, pink when young, chocolate brown in age. Stem with prominent ring. Caps attached to stem in ball and socket fashion. Habitat on ground.	**Coprinaceae**  *Coprinus:* Caps smooth or scaly. Gills crowded, soon dissolving or becoming paper thin. Habitat varied.
SLIM STEMS; texture different from cap	**Strophariaceae** *Psilocybe:* Caps conic, convex, or plane, with or without umbo. Veil persistent, disappearing, or absent. Habitat in soil, grass, dung, or wood debris.	 *Panaeolus:* Caps parabolic, convex, or campanulate. Gills mottled from uneven ripening of spores. Stems with or without ring. Habitat on dung, in grass, or in rich soil.
GILLS ATTACHED; cap and stem of similar texture	*Naematoloma:* Caps yellow to reddish or orangish yellow. Gills purplish in age. Veil often leaving remnants on margin. Common species tufted on rotting wood.  *Stropharia:* Caps ± slimy or sticky. Ring on stem in many species. Habitat varied.	*Psathyrella:* Caps dull colored, striate when wet. Stems fragile, often brittle with a rind, whitish, occasionally with a ring. Habitat on wood or ground. **Gomphidiaceae** Gills decurrent, distant, and waxy. Stem often with annular zone. *Gomphidius:* Cap viscid and flesh whitish. Young gills and flesh whitish. Stem base often yellow. *Chroogomphus:* Young gills and flesh colored from start.

Generic Key to the Dark Brown to Black Spored Agarics

This key can be used to determine the genus of mushroom species with dark brown the purplish brown or black spore deposits. *It does not apply to the rust brown, dull brown, or yellowish brown spored mushrooms.* After keying out a collection, refer to the notes at the end of this key.

1a Gills deliquescing ('melting'), or becoming paper thin at maturity. . . . . *Coprinus*
1b Gills not as above. **2**

2a Partial veil membranous (sometimes floccose), often leaving a membranous annulus on the stem. **3**
2b Partial veil not membranous, membranous annulus never present. **5**

3a Gills free. Spore deposit typically chocolate brown. . . . . *Agaricus*
3b Gills attached (unless seceding). Spore deposit not as above. **4**

4a Spore deposit typically black. (Cap cuticle cellular.) . . . . *Psathyrella*
4b Spore deposit typically purplish brown to very dark purplish brown. (Cap cuticle filamentous.) . . . . *Stropharia*
4c Spore deposit typically lighter, cinnamon brown to earth brown. (Cap cuticle cellular or filamentous.) . . . . see *Agrocybe* and *Pholiota*

5a Gills decurrent, thick, and waxy. **6**
5b Gills subdecurrent, adnate, adnexed, sinuate, seceding, or uncinate, but generally not decurrent, not thick, and rarely waxy. **7**

6a Cap surface extremely viscid to glutinous when moist. Pellicle and partial veil thickly gelatinous. Cap flesh whitish, not bluing in Melzer's iodine. . . . . *Gomphidius*
6b Cap surface dry, sometimes viscid when moist. Partial veil not gelatinous. Cap flesh colored, bluing in Melzer's iodine. . . . . *Chroogomphus*

7a Typically growing in dung, in well manured grounds, or in rich grassy areas. **8**
7b Typically growing in decayed wood substratum, on decaying logs and stumps, in wood chips and bark mulch, etc. **11**

8a Spore deposit blackish. Cap usually not viscid when moist and lacking a separable gelatinous pellicle. **9**
8b Spore deposit purplish brown. Cap generally viscid when moist in most species and having a seperable gelatinous pellicle. **10**

9a Gills soon becoming mottled from uneven ripening of the spores (often not seen when fully mature.) (Spores not fading in concentrated sulphuric acid.) . . . . *Panaeolus*

9b Gills not becoming mottled. (Spores fading in concentrated sulphuric acid.) . . . . *Psathyrella*

10a Cap generally brownish when moist in fresh fruiting bodies and very hygrophanous (markedly fading in coloration upon drying.) Some species bruise bluish green. (Chrysocystidia always absent.) . . . . *Psilocybe*

10b Cap generally yellowish when moist in fresh fruiting bodies and usually not very hygrophanous (not markedly fading in coloration upon drying.) Species not bruising bluish green. (Chrysocystidia present, or if absent stem must be viscid to glutinous.) . . . . *Stropharia*

11a Cap generally colored in yellows, oranges, or reds. Typically not very hygrophanous. . . . . *Naematoloma*

11b Cap generally colored in browns. Typically hygrophanous. **12**

12a Cap often viscid when moist from a gelatinous pellicle, separable in many species. Stem and cap sometimes bruising bluish green. Cap pliant, not truly brittle when squeezed. (Cap cuticle filamentous.) . . . . *Psilocybe*

12b Cap usually not viscid when moist and lacking a separable gelatinous pellicle. Stem and cap never bruising bluish green. Cap brittle when squeezed. (Cap cuticle cellular.) . . . . *Psathyrella*

NOTES

The following genera are included in these families:

Naematoloma, Psilocybe, Stropharia . . . . Strophariaceae
Panaeolus, Psathyrella, Coprinus. . . . . Coprinaceae
Chroogomphus, Gomphidius. . . . . Gomphidiaceae
Agaricus. . . . . Agaricaceae
Agrocybe (with *Conocybe* and *Bolbitius*). . . . . Bolbitiaceae
Pholiota (with *Cortinarius, Galerina, Gymnopilus,*
    Hebeloma, Inocybe and others) . . . . Cortinariaceae

When keying out a mushroom collection to *Naematoloma, Psilocybe,* or *Stropharia,* turn to the Key to the Family Strophariaceae.

When keying out a mushroom collection to *Panaeolus,* turn to the Key to the Genus Panaeolus.

When keying out a mushroom collection to other genera, consult the texts in the Annotated Bibliography of General Mushroom Field Guides.

EXCEPTIONS TO THIS KEY

A few species exhibiting features uncharacteristic of their genus can cause difficulty for people using this key. They are outlined below.

Stropharia kauffmanii has an 'army' brown spore deposit and should key out to **4b** instead of **4c**.

Naematoloma elongatum has a cinnamon brown spore deposit.

Panaeolus foenisecii (also known as *Panaeolina foenisecii*) has a deep brown spore deposit, not black or violet-black as is typical of all other panaeoli.

Panaeolus semiovatus is unusual because of its viscid cap and the presence of a membranous annulus on the stem. This species would mistakenly be keyed out under *Stropharia.*

Two eastern panaeoli, *Panaeolus fontinalis* and *Panaeolus fraxinophilus,* grow in rich humus of swamps or on decaying logs of ash, respectively. All other panaeoli grow in dung or in grassy habitats.

Key to the Strophariaceae (North American Species)

This key is based on features characteristic of species in *Naematoloma, Psilocybe,* and *Stropharia.* The key works best when using fresh specimens encompassing the entire fruiting cycle, from the earliest stages of development to the most mature. Be sure the mushrooms in question belong to this family by 1) taking a spore print and determining it to be purplish gray to purplish brown to black and 2) keying out the collection to one of the previously mentioned genera using both Diagram D and the Generic Key to the Dark Brown to Black Spored Agarics.

Geographically, this key encompasses the continental United States and Canada. Most species can be found in coastal and mountainous regions of western North America though many species are common across the continent. Mushrooms having a tendency to exhibit significantly variable features are keyed out more than once to insure the user is not misled. In key leads where species are very closely related, the delineating microscopic features (measured in microns or μ) have been included in parentheses. Upon keying out a collection to species, compare the description and/or photograph with the actual mushrooms and note that closely related species are suggested as alternative possibilities. Take your time, good luck, and happy hunting.

1a Well-formed and fairly persistent membranous annulus present. **2**
1b Membranous annulus poorly developed or entirely absent. **22**

2a Cap bluish when moist in fresh collections *and* strophariod in stature. **3**

2b Not as above. **4**

3a Cap up to 7 cm broad when fully mature, greenish to bluish
overall in color, sometimes with yellowish patches in drying.
Stem often viscid when wet. . . . . *Stropharia aeruginosa* complex

3b Cap up to 3(4) cm broad when fully mature, pale whitish to
yellowish overall in color, usually with slight bluish tints.
Stem dry or moist when wet, not viscid. . . . . *Stropharia albocyanea*

4a Stem initially covered with conspicuous cottony scales to the
annulus. Cap also frequently adorned with scales, especially
along the margin, though often absent in age. **5**

4b Stem and cap smooth or covered with fine fibrillose zones,
but free of distinct scales. **11**

5a Stem viscid when moist. Common only in the eastern or
southeastern United States. . . . . *Stropharia hardii*

5b Stem not viscid when moist. Common *not* only in the
eastern or southeastern United States. **6**

6a Cap viscid when moist in fresh specimens from a gelatinous
pellicle that is that is often separable. **7**

6b Cap not distinctly viscid when moist and lacking a
gelatinous pellicle. **10**

7a Cap brick red to scarlet red. **8**

7b Cap not as above. **9**

8a Stem pallid to brownish towards the base. (Chrysocystidia
absent.) . . . . *Psilocybe thrausta*

8b Stem yellowish to reddish towards the base. (Chrysocystidia
present.) . . . . *Naematoloma aurantiaca*

9a Cap extremely viscid to glutinous when moist and
hygrophanous (markedly fading in color upon drying.)
Rhizomorphs at base of stem whitish. . . . . *Stropharia hornemannii*

9b Cap viscid when moist but not as above, not particularly
hygrophanous. Rhizomorphs at base of stem orange
buff. . . . . *Psilocybe squamosa*

10a Membranous annulus with pronounced 'gills' on its
upper side . Cap more reddish, especially when
young. . . . . see *Stropharia rugoso-annulata*

10b Membranous annulus smooth or striate but not as above.
Cap more yellowish brown. . . . . *Stropharia kauffmanii*

11a Upperside of annulus with raised 'gills'. **12**

11b Upperside of annulus relatively smooth or only striate, but
not as above. **13**

12a Cap 4.5–13 cm broad; reddish to reddish brown in color, especially when young. Typically growing in cultivated grounds and gardens. . . . . *Stropharia rugoso-annulata*

12b Cap 2.5–5 cm broad; yellowish to whitish in color. Typically growing in grassy areas. . . . . *Stropharia bilamellata*

13a Mushrooms pallid to yellowish overall with slight bluish tints that are not a product of bruising. . . . . *Stropharia albocyanea*

13b Not as above. **14**

14a Stem (and cap) bruising bluish green with time. **15**

14a Stem (and cap) not bruising bluish green with time. **18**

15a Partial veil thinly membranous, leaving a non-persistent membranous annulus soon deteriorating into a fibrillose annular zone. Cap margin markedly translucent-striate when moist in fresh specimens. Common to the Pacific Northwest. . . . . *Psilocybe stuntzii* group

15b Partial veil generally thickly membranous, leaving a fairly persistent membranous annulus. Cap margin not markedly translucent-striate when moist in fresh specimens. Not common to the Pacific Northwest. **16**

16a Cap generally greater than 4 cm broad when fully mature. Distributed throughout the southeastern United States as far west as Texas and North to Tennessee. . . . . *Psilocybe cubensis*

16b Cap generally less than 4 (5) cm broad when fully mature. Reported only from California. **17**

17a Cap whitish to smoky brown towards the center; not distinctly viscid when moist. (Chrysocystidia absent.) . . . . *Psilocybe sp.*

17b Cap brownish to yellowish brown overall; distinctly viscid when moist from a gelatinous pellicle. (Chrysocystidia present.) . . . . *Naematoloma popperianum*

18a Cap scarlet red to brick red in color. . . . . see *Naematoloma aurantiaca*

18b Cap not as above. **19**

19a Cap whitish overall in color. . . . . *Stropharia albonitens.*

19b Cap more yellowish in color. **20**

20a Gills brownish when mature. Growing in sandy soils of river flats, often under alder. . . . . *Stropharia magnivelaris*

20b Gills purplish brown to violet when mature. Growth habitat not as above. **21**

21a Growing mostly in grass. (Spores 7–9.5 x 4.5 μ.) . . . . *Stropharia coronilla*

21b Growing mostly in dung or in well manured grounds. (Spores 12 x 7–8 μ.) . . . . *Stropharia melanosperma*

22a Cap bright bluish green to bluish in fresh collections
(*not* a product of bruising). . . . . *Stropharia aeruginosa* complex

22b Cap not as above. **23**

23a Cap distinctly reddish in color. **24**

23b Cap not as above. **26**

24a Partial veil membranous, best seen in very young well-
preserved specimens. . . . . *Naematoloma aurantiaca*

24b Partial veil cortinate, thin to obscure, best seen in very
young well-preserved specimens. **25**

25a Cap 2–8 cm in diameter at maturity. Margin not
translucent-striate when moist. Surface only moist
when wet. . . . . *Naematoloma sublateritium*

25b Cap .5–1.5 (2) cm in diameter at maturity. Martin distinctly
translucent-striate when moist. Surface subviscid
when wet. . . . . see *Psilocybe subviscida*

26a Stem extremely viscid to glutinous below the annular zone
when moist in fresh specimens. Partial veil glutinous (seen
only in the youngest of fruiting bodies). **27**

26b Stem and partial veil not as above. **28**

27a Growing in dung or in well manured grounds. Stem
generally not tapering into a pseudorhiza. . . . . *Stropharia semiglobata*

27b Growing in humus rich in lignin, often under spruce. Stem
often tapering into a long pseudorhiza. . . . . *Stropharia semigloboides*

28a Cap viscid when moist from a gelatinous pellicle that is
usually separable in fresh collections. **29**

28b Cap not distinctly viscid when moist and lacking a
gelatinous pellicle in fresh collections. **63**

29a Stem (and cap) distinctly bruising bluish green in time. **30**

29b Stem (and cap) not bruising bluish green in time. **41**

30a Cap conic to conic-campanulate to campanulate, sometimes
expanding to convex, but typically not expanding further
at maturity. **31**

30b Cap soon expanding to broadly covex to plane with age. **36**

31a Gills purplish brown at full maturity. Most commonly found
growing in grassy areas (lawns, fields, etc.) on or about piles
of dung. . . . . *Psilocybe semilanceata*

31b Gills dull brownish at full maturity. Most commonly found
in decayed wood substratum, sometimes in newly laid lawns
or in the field-forest interface. **32**

32a Margin undulated and often very irregular when conic
to convex. **33**

32b Margin straight or nearly so when conic to convex. **35**

33a Diameter of cap to length of stem ratio near .30 in mature specimens. Rhizomorphs typically absent from base of stem. . . . . see *Psilocybe strictipes*

33b Diameter of cap to length of stem ratio near .60 (or greater) in mature specimens. Rhizomorphs typically present at base of stem **34**

34a Partial veil thinly cortinate to obscure or absent. Gelatinous pellicle easily separable in fresh collections. Known from northern California to British Columbia. . . . . *Psilocybe baeocystis*

34b Partial veil copiously cortinate. Gelatinous pellicle generally barely separable in fresh collections. Known from the from the southeastern United States. . . . . *Psilocybe caerulescens* complex

35a Known only from the Pacific Northwest (including northern California). (Spores 9–13 5–7 μ.) . . . . *Psilocybe pelliculosa*

35b Known from both the northwestern and northeastern United States (Michigan to New York to Ontario). (Spores 6–9.5 (11.5) x 4.5–5.5 μ.) . . . . *Psilocybe silvatica*

36a Partial veil thinly membranous, leaving a non-persistent membranous annulus that soon deteriorates into a fairly persistent annular zone of fibrils on the stem. . . . . . . *Psilocybe stuntzii* group

36b Partial veil not membranous but cortinate to absent, sometimes leaving a slight, non-persistent annular zone of fibrils on the stem, if at all. **37**

37a Cap margin typically straight or nearly so when conic to convex. **38**

37b Cap margin typically undulated when conic to convex. **39**

38a Stem yellowish brown overall. Cap margin typically incurved at first. Reported from Quebec in decayed wood substratum of alder, birch, fir, and spruce. . . . . *Psilocybe quebecensis*

38b Stem whitish overall (except when bluing). Cap margin not typically incurved at first. Reported from the northwestern United States in decayed wood substratum of mostly cedar and fir, sometimes in grassy areas where wood is buried underneath (i.e., newly laid lawns, etc.). . . . . *Psilocybe cyanescens*

39a Growing in decayed hardwood substratum, particularly birch and maple. Bruising bluish green with time. Widely distributed throughout the midwestern United States, from Maine to North Carolina to Tennessee to Michigan. . . . . . *Psilocybe caerulipes*

39b Growing in decayed conifer substratum, in wood chips or bark mulch, in newly laid lawns, or in the field-forest

interface. Quickly bruising bluish green. Common to the
northwestern United States and British Columbia. **40**

40a Diameter of cap to length of stem ratio generally near .30 in
mature specimens. Rhizomorphs typically absent from base
of stem. (Cheilocystidia 26–45 x 6–12 μ.) . . . . *Psilocybe strictipes*

40b Diameter of cap to length of stem ratio generally near .60 in
mature specimens. Rhizomorphs typically present about base
of stem. (Cheilocystidia 20–30 (36) x 4–6 μ.) . . . . *Psilocybe baeocystis*

41a Cap whitish to yellowish to orangish when moist in fresh
collections; not particularly hygrophanous. **42**

41b Cap more brownish when moist in fresh collections; usually
very hygrophanous. **50**

42a Typically growing in cespitose clusters. **43**

42b Typically growing scattered to gregariously. **44**

43a Gills distinctly tinted greenish at maturity. Taste
bitter. . . . . see *Naematoloma fasciculare*

43b Gills pallid cinnamon brown at maturity and without
greenish tones. Taste mild. . . . . *Naematoloma subochraceum*

44a Growing in decayed wood substratum and/or in sandy soils
of river flats. **45**

44b Growing in grassy areas, in well manured grounds, and in
dung. **47**

45a Cap whitish overall and generally not greater than 3 cm
broad at maturity. . . . . see *Stropharia albonitens*

45b Cap more yellowish overall and generally greater than 3 cm
broad at maturity. **46**

46a Cap pale yellow to bright yellow. Gills dark purplish brown
at maturity. Growing mostly in the fall and to a lesser degree
in the spring. . . . . *Stropharia ambigua*

46b Cap pale grayish yellow. Gills browish at maturity. Reported
to be growing only in the spring. . . . . *Stropharia magnivelaris*

47a Cap whitish overall. . . . . *Stropharia albonitens*

47b Cap more yellowish overall. **48**

48a Cap typically furnished with a distinct umbo when mature.
(Basidia 2–spored.) . . . . *Psilocybe umbonatescens*

48b Cap typically not furnished with an umbo. (Basidia 4–spored.) **49**

49a Gills brownish when fully mature. Stem flocculose above the
annular zone (if present), dry, and in many collections
tapering into a long pseudorhiza. (Spores 12–15 x
7–9 μ.) . . . . *Stropharia siccipes*

49b Gills dark purplish brown (often with a slight olive cast) when fully mature. Stem smooth above the annular zone (if present), subviscid when moist, and not tapering into a long pseudorhiza. (Spores 16–20 x 10–12 μ.) . . . . *Stropharia stercoraria*

50a Cap conic to obtusely conic to campanulate, occasionally convex but not expanding further. **51**

50b Cap convex, soon expanding to broadly convex to nearly plane or flattened when fully mature. **59**

51a Commonly found in grassy areas, in well manured grounds, and in dung. **52**

51b Commonly found in decayed wood substratum. **55**

52a Cap 2–6 mm broad. Usually in the dung of wild animals such as elk, marmots, etc. . . . . *Psilocybe angustispora*

52b Cap 5–40 mm broad. Usually growing in damp grassy areas and in the dung of domesticated animals. **53**

53a Stem 4–14 cm long at maturity, often flexuous. Cap tending to conic or conic-campanulate with an acute umbo. Gill attachment adnexed or ascending. . . . . *Psilocybe semilanceata*

53b Stem generally shorter at maturity, usually straight unless curved at the base. Cap tending to convex to broadly convex, usually without an acute umbo. Gill attachment adnate to subdecurrent. **54**

54a Fibrillose annular zone present on the stem, soon darkened by spores. . . . . see *Psilocybe merdaria* complex

54b Fibrillose annular zone not present on the stem. . . . . see *Psilocybe coprophila* complex

55a Cap markedly translucent-striate most of the way to the disc in moist, fresh specimens. (This character is lost in drying.) **56**

55b Cap not as above, shortly translucent-striate only along the margin. **57**

56a Known only from the western United States and western Canada. (Spores 9–13 x 5–7 μ.) . . . . see *Psilocybe pelliculosa*

56b Known from the northwestern and northeastern United States and eastern Canada. (Spores 6–9.5 (11.5) x 4.5–5.5 μ.) . . . . see *Psilocybe silvatica*

57a Typically growing in cespitose clusters. . . . . *Naematoloma dispersum* var. *idahoense*

57b Typically growing scattered to gregariously. **58**

58a Base of stem becoming dark reddish brown but not distinctly blackening with age. In drying, cap becoming

orangish yellow-brown from the disc. Cap flesh dingy white
to olive. (Chrysocystidia present.) . . . . . . *Naematoloma dispersum* var. *typica*

58b Base of stem distinctly blackening with age. In drying, cap
becoming dull cinnamon to pale pecan from the disc. Cap
flesh dark reddish brown (when moist) to pallid tan (when
dry). (Chrysocystidia absent.). . . . . *Psilocybe washingtonensis*

59a Annular zone of fibrils present on the stem. **60**
59b Annular zone absent. **62**

60a Fruiting bodies large, caps measuring 5 cm or greater in
breadth at maturity. Stem covered by fragile whitish scales in
young specimens, soon disappearing. . . . . *Stropharia hornemannii*
60b Fruiting bodies small, caps measuring less than 5 cm in
breadth at maturity. Stem may be covered with fine
fibrillose zones but always free of distinct scales. **61**

61a Stem 2–4 cm long when mature. Typically growing in
dung. . . . . *Psilocybe merdaria* complex
61b Stem 4–8 (13) cm long when mature. Typically growing in
low damp areas but not in dung. . . . . *Naematoloma ericaeum*

62a Growing in grassy areas, in lawns, and beside roadsides.
Stem often flexuous. . . . . *Psilocybe californica*
62b Growing only in dung, or in well manured grounds. Stem
straight overall or curved just at the base. . . . . . *Psilocybe coprophila* complex

63a Species semitropical. Stem (and cap) readily bruising bluish
green, tapering into a long pseudorhiza in many collections,
and having long whitish rhizomorphs protruding about the
base. . . . . *Psilocybe caerulescens* complex
63b Not as above. **64**

64a Cap with distinct olive greenish casts (not a product of
bruising) **65**
64b Cap without olive greenish casts. **66**

65a Typically growing in cespitose clusters. Gill with strong
greenish hues at maturity. Growing on wood or in decayed
wood substratum. . . . . *Naematoloma fasciculare*
65b Typically growing scattered to gregariously but not in
cespitose clusters. Gills with slight greenish hues at maturity.
Growing in rich humus or in the outwashes of
streams. . . . . *Naematoloma olivaceotinctum*

66a Stem covered by floccose recurved scales. Typically growing
in deciduous forests. . . . . see *Stropharia kauffmanii*
66b Stem free of scales. Typically *not* growing in deciduous
forests. **67**

67a Cap yellowish to orangish yellow when moist in fresh
fruiting bodies, usually not very hygrophanous. **68**
67b Cap brownish to orangish brown when moist in fresh
fruiting bodies, usually very hygrophanous. **72**

68a Typically growing in cespitose clusters. **69**
68b Typically growing scattered to gregariously. **70**

69a Gills yellowish brown with distinct greenish casts at
maturity. Taste bitter. . . . . *Naematoloma fasciculare*
69b Gills smoky brown at maturity. Taste not
bitter. . . . . *Naematoloma capnoides*

70a Stem blackening from the base upwards in age.
(Chrysocystidia absent.) . . . . *Psilocybe corneipes*
70b Stem not as above. (Chrysocystidia present.) **71**

71a Gills becoming purplish brown at maturity. Spore deposit
dark purplish brown. . . . . *Naematoloma udum*
71b Gills becoming sordid brown at maturity. Spore deposit dull
cinnamon brown. . . . . *Naematoloma elongatum*

72a Most commonly found growing in cespitose clusters. **73**
72b Most commonly growing scattered to gregariously. **74**

73a Cap tending to readily expand to plane and often uplifted
in age. Gills purplish brown at maturity. . . . . *Naematoloma squalidellum*
73b Cap tending to expand only to convex or broadly convex in
age. Gills sordid grayish brown at
maturity. . . . .*Naematoloma dispersum* var. *idahoense*

74a Stem usually flexuous and concolorous with cap in fresh
specimens. . . . . *Psilocybe montana*
74b Stem usually straight or nearly so, sometimes curved at the
base, and generally not concolorous with the cap in fresh
specimens. **75**

75a Typically growing in dung. Fibrillose annular zone present,
generally not superior but located in the median to lower
regions of the stem in mature specimens. . . . . . . *Psilocybe merdaria* complex
75b Typically *not* growing in dung. Annular zone, if present,
superior in mature specimens. **76**

76a Cap margin initially appressed against the stem. Growing in
low damp grassy areas, often under
pine. . . . . *Naematoloma ericaeum*
76b Cap margin initially not appressed against the stem.
Growing in decayed wood substratum, in mossy
areas, etc. **77**

77a Cap tending to remain convex and not expanding further
upon maturity. . . . . see *Naematoloma dispersum* var. *typica*
77b Cap tending to expand to nearly plane or flattened upon
maturity. **78**

78a Taste bitter. Known only from the eastern United States.
(Spores 14–18 (20) x 5–7 μ.) . . . . *Naematoloma udum*
78b Taste not bitter. Known from both the eastern and western
United States. (Spores smaller.) **79**

79a Cap generally not greater than 2.5 cm broad when fully
mature. (Spores 7–9 x 3.5–4 (4.5) μ.) . . . . *Naematoloma polytrichi*
79b Cap generally greater than 2.5 cm broad at maturity.
(Spores (8) 9–11 (12) x (4) 5–6 μ.) . . . . *Naematoloma squalidellum*

Key to the Genus *Panaeolus* (North American Species)

When using this key, it is essential to work from fresh representative collections encompassing the entire fruiting cycle. If you only have one or two poorly preserved specimens, it is best to discard them. Be sure the mushrooms in question belong to this genus by 1) taking a spore print and determining it to be black or nearly so* and 2) keying out the collection to *Panaeolus* using both Diagram D and the Generic Key to the Dark Brown to Black Spored Agarics. Upon keying out a collection to species, compare the description and/or photograph with the actual specimens and note that closely related panaeoli are often suggested as alternative possibilities. Good luck and happy hunting.

1a Membranous annulus typically present on the stem.
(Sometimes this deteriorates into a fibrillose annular
zone.) . . . . *Panaeolus semiovatus*
1b Membranous annulus always absent. **2**

2a Cap margin appendiculate with distinct floccose remnants of
the partial veil, often 'tooth-like' in appearance and best seen
in fresh young specimens. **3**
2b Cap margin lacking remnants of the partial veil. **7**

3a Cap surface markedly reticulate with dark interconnecting
veins radiating outwards from the disc. . . . . *Panaeolus retirugis*
3b Cap not as above. **4**

4a Caps pallid to whitish overall. **5**
4b Caps brownish to grayish brown overall. **6**

*Panaeolus foenisceii is the one exception to this rule. It has a dark brown spore deposit.

5a Cap 2–4 cm broad at maturity, soon becoming horizontally cracked or scaly. (Pleurocystidia absent.) . . . . *Panaeolus papilionaceus*

5b Cap 4–10 cm broad at maturity, sometimes wrinkled in age but generally not cracked or scaly. (Pleurocystidia present.) . . . . *Panaeolus phalaenarum*

6a Caps grayish brown often with slight olivaceous tones. . . . . *Panaeolus sphinctrinus**

6b Caps brown with distinct reddish tones. . . . . *Panaeolus campanulatus**

7a Flesh of cap and/or stem bruising bluish green. **8**

7b Not as above. **11**

8a Rapidly bruising bluish green where touched. Species generally tropical to subtropical. Reported from Hawaii, southern California, Florida, and elsewhere in the southeastern United States. **9**

8b Weakly bruising bluish green, usually over a period of time and mostly at the stem base. Species temperate, occasionally subtropical. Reported across much of the North American continent. **10**

9a (Spores 12–14 x 8.5–11 μ.) . . . . *Panaeolus cyanescens*

9b (Spores 10.5–12 x 7–9 μ.) . . . . *Panaeolus tropicalis*

10a Cap soon expanding to plane, often with a broad umbo. (Germ pore central.) . . . . *Panaeolus subbalteatus*

10b Cap expanding to convex or broadly convex but not as above. (Germ pore eccentric.) . . . . *Panaeolus sp.*

11a Growing on decaying logs and stumps or in humus rich in lignin content (woody tissue). **12**

11b Growing in dung, in well manured grounds, or in grassy areas. **13**

12a Growing on logs of fallen ash trees. Cap flesh darkened in moist fresh specimens. Gills dull grayish brown when immature, without olivaceous hues. . . . . *Panaeolus fraxinophilus*

12b Growing in the rich humus of swamps. Cap flesh pallid in moist fresh specimens. Gills yellowish brown or brownish with distinct olivaceous hues. . . . . *Panaeolus fontinalis*

13a Cap furnished with a pronounced dark band along the margin, especially apparent when partially dry. **14**

13b Cap not as above. **18**

14a Typically growing in cespitose clusters. Cap readily expanding to plane in age. see *Panaeolus subbalteatus*

*These two species comprise a complex of very closely related mushrooms.

14b Typically growing scattered to gregariously. Cap tending to remain campanulate to convex, rarely expanding further. **15**

15a Cap dingy gray to dark gray to gray-black when moist. (Pleurocystidia present, though few in numbers [excluding chrysocystidia]). . . . . *Panaeolus fimicola*

15b Cap pinkish cinnamon to cinnamon brown to chestnut when moist. (Pleurocystidia absent [excluding chrysocystidia]). **16**

16a Gills dark brown at maturity. Spore deposit dark brown to very dark cinnamon brown. . . . . *Panaeolus foenisecii*

16b Gills dark purplish gray-black at maturity. Spore deposit black or nearly so. **17**

17a Cap conic at first, often becoming convex to plane in age. Cap 2.5–5.0 cm broad at maturity. . . . . *Panaeolus acuminatus* *

17b Cap parabolic at first, never expanding to plane, becoming campanulate in age. Cap .5–2.0 cm broad at maturity . . . *Panaeolus rickenii* *

18a Caps pallid to whitish overall when moist. Frequently growing in cespitose or subcespitose clusters. **19**

18b Caps more brownish overall when moist. Frequently growing scattered to gregariously. **20**

19a Stem solid. (Spores 18–22 x 11–12.5 μ.) . . . . *Panaeolus phalaenarum*

19b Stem soon becoming tubular. (Spores (10) 12–14 (15) x (6) 8–9 (10) μ.) . . . . see *Panaeolus sp.*

20a Spore deposit and gills at maturity dark brown. . . . . *Panaeolus foenisecii*

20b Spore deposit and gills at maturity dark purplish brown to black. **21**

21a Cap remaining reddish brown on the disc while becoming lighter in coloration towards the margin in drying. Cap margin usually not distinctly translucent-striate in moist fresh specimens. (Spores finely roughened.) . . . . *Panaeolus castaneifolius*

21b Cap fading from the disc while becoming darker in coloration towards the margin in drying. Cap margin often translucent-striate in moist fresh specimens. (Spores smooth.) **22**

22a Cap conic at first, characteristically convex to plane in age. . . . . *Panaeolus acuminatus* *

22b Cap parabolic at first, characteristically campanulate in age. . . . . *Panaeolus rickenii* *

*These two species comprise a complex of very closely related mushrooms.

4 | Species Descriptions

THE GENUS *CONOCYBE* FAYOD

Conocybe typically grows scattered to gregariously and has a long thin fragile stem. The habitats in which this genus grows varies from dung and grass to decayed wood substratum. Species of *Conocybe* that have a well developed partial veil are placed into the sub-genus *Pholiotina* following Dr. Rolf Singer. *Pholiotina filaris (Conocybe filaris)* is known to contain toxins similar to those found in the most deadly of amanitas and galerinas.

It is not very difficult for one to confuse wood or moss inhabiting species of *Conocybe* with some species of *Galerina*. A sure way for telling *Galerina* from *Conocybe* is by the microscopic nature of the cap cuticle. Galerinas (and psilocybes) have filamentous cap cuticles whereas conocybes (and panaeoli) generally have cap cuticles composed of inflated rounded cells. To a certain degree, one can determine visually whether a mushroom has a filamentous or cellular cap cuticle by the reflective quality of the cap in moist, fresh specimens.

Two species of this genus, *Conocybe cyanopus* and *Conocybe smithii*, are known to be hallucinogenic. With time, they both bruise bluish green (though sometimes not markedly so), usually just at the base of the stem. In view of the existence of *Conocybe filaris* and its non-persistent annulus, I strongly discourage amateurs from experimenting with species of *Conocybe*. There are an abundance of other dark purplish brown spored psilocybian species that do not present the dangers of this genus.

» C. cyanopus (ATKINS) KUHNER

Cap: .7–1.2 (2.5) cm broad. Nearly hemispheric to convex, expanding to broadly convex with age. Margin translucent-striate when moist and often appendiculate at first with minute fibrillose remnants of the partial veil. Reddish cinnamon brown to dark brown. Surface moist when wet, soon dry; smooth overall to slightly wrinkled towards the disc.

Gills: Attachment adnexed, close, and moderately broad. Dull rusty brown with a whitish fringe along the margin.

Stem: 2–4 cm long by 1–1.4 mm thick. Equal to slightly curved at the base, and fragile. Whitish at first, becoming grayish or brownish at the apex, and often bluish green at the base. Partial veil thinly cortinate, often leaving trace remnants along the cap margin, soon disappearing.

Growth habit and habitat: Scattered in grassy areas, in lawns, and fields in the summer and fall. Reported from Washington; Vancouver, B.C.; and Colorado.

Comments: Hallucinogenic, containing psilocybin and/or psilocin. This species is probably widely distributed across the continent. See also *Conocybe filaris* and *Conocybe smithii.*

Microscopic characters: (Spores 6.5–7.5 (8.5) x 4.5–5 μ. Basidia 4-spored. Pleurocystidia absent. Cheilocystidia present, 20–25 x 7.5–10 μ.

» *C. filaris* FRIES

Cap: .5–2.5 cm broad. Obtusely conic at first, soon expanding to conic-convex or convex-campanulate, then nearly plane and often with a pronounced but broad umbo. Margin slightly translucent-striate when moist. Orangish tawny brown. Surface moist when wet, soon dry, usually smooth overall.

Gills: Attachment adnexed, close, moderately broad, and with one to three tiers of intermediate gills. Rusty brown at maturity.

Stem: 1–4 cm long by 1–2 mm thick. Stem fibrous, equal to slightly enlarged upwards, and often curved at the base. Dingy yellowish brown to ochraceous. Partial veil membranous, leaving a fragile non-persistent, *movable,* membranous annulus colored rusty brown by spores in the median to lower region of the stem.

Growth habit and habitat: Scattered to gregarious in decayed wood substratum, in wood or bark chips, or on newly laid lawns and grassy areas. Reported throughout the northwest and suspected to be widely distributed across the continent.

Comments: Also known as *Pholiotina filaris* (Fries) Singer. There are several closely related species which make up the *Conocybe filaris* complex. *Conocybe filaris* has been reported to contain the same deadly amatoxins as *Amanita phalloides* and *Galerina autumnalis.* The non-persistent nature of the annulus brings the appearance of this mushroom very close to that of other conocybes.

Microscopic characters: Spores 7.5–13 x 3.5–6.5 μ. Basidia 2-and 4-spored. Pleurocystidia absent.

» *C. smithii* WATLING

Cap: 3–1.0(1.3) cm broad. Obtusely conic, expanding to nearly plane with a distinct pronounced umbo. Margin translucent-striate most the way to disc when moist. Ochraceous tawny to cinnamon brown, hygrophanous, becoming pale pinkish yellow in drying.

Gills: Adnate to adnexed, soon seceding, crowded to subdistant, narrow to moderately broad. Pale grayish yellow at first, becoming rusty cinnamon brown at maturity.

Stem: 1–5(7) cm long by .75–1.0(1.5) mm thick. Equal to slightly enlarged at the base, fragile. Whitish becoming slightly pallid yellowish brown, and more grayish at the base. Surface covered with fine fibrils at first but soon smooth overall. Partial veil thin to absent.

Growth habit and habitat: Scattered to numerous in moss in and about sphagnum bogs, and in damp wet places. Reported from Washington and Michigan.

Comments: Hallucinogenic, containing psilocybin and/or psilocin. The range of this species is likely to be much more extensive than the literature presently indicates. See also *Conocybe filaris* and *Conocybe cyanopus.*

Microscopic characters: Spores (6.5) 7–9 x 4–4.5(5) μ. Basidia 4-spored. Pleurocystidia absent. Cheilocystidia 20–40 x 9–15 μ.

THE GENUS *GALERINA* EARLE

Galerinas often grow in cespitose clusters on decaying logs or in moss and have relatively short brittle stems. Microscopically, the cap cuticle is filamentous and the spores have a lens-shaped depression near the apices. Galerinas may or may not have a partial veil that leaves a membranous annulus or fibrillous annular zone. The gills are rust brown at spore maturity. Species in the section *Naucoriopsis* are known to be deadly poisonous and the aspect of *Galerina autumnalis* can be very similar to *Psilocybe stuntzii*. Also there is a great deal of similarity between mycenoid galerinas and *Psilocybe pelliculosa*.

Galerina marginata (as *Pholiota marginata*) was first reported to be edible and of 'excellent quality' by the reknowned C.M. McIlvaine in his book *One Thousand American Fungi*. In his time little was known about the edibility of mushrooms and he would daringly eat many of the species he encountered. It is now known that a race (or strain) of *Galerina marginata* can be extremely poisonous, sometimes resulting in death. To further confuse matters, there are at least 199 recognized species of *Galerina*, many of which can only be distinguished microscopically. For this reason, most mycologists upon sight identification will place a species such as this into a group of closely related mushrooms as in the '*Galerina autumnalis* complex'. Learn to recognize the *Galerina* species and avoid them.

» *G. autumnalis*
(PECK) SMITH AND SINGER

Cap: 1–5(6.5) cm broad. Convex to broadly convex, soon expanding with age to plane, often with an elevated and undulated margin and with a low broad umbo. Margin translucent-striate when moist. Dull yellowish brown to orangish brown to cinnamon or reddish cinnamon brown when moist, hygrophanous, fading to dingy yellowish in drying. Surface slightly viscid to viscid when moist from a gelatinous pellicle, sometimes separable. Flesh relatively thin at the margin and thicker towards the disc.

Gills: Attachment adnate to uncinate, sometimes seceding, close to subdistant, and moderately broad. Golden yellowish brown becoming dull cinnamon to nearly concolorous with the cap at maturity.

Stem: (3)5–9 cm long by (3)4–8 mm thick. Equal to slightly enlarged at the base and hollow. Grayish brown overall and darkening from the base upwards. Surface slightly fibrillose, becoming smooth, and often longitudinally striate. Partial veil thinly membranous, leaving a small fragile membranous annulus which soon deteriorates into a fairly persistent annular zone of fibrils.

Growth habit and habitat: Growing scattered to gregarious or cespitose on decayed conifer and hardwood logs or debris, in wood chips or bark mulch, or in newly laid lawns in the fall throughout the United States and Canada.

Comments: The species within this complex are known to be deadly poisonous. They are similar in their aspect to *Psilocybe stuntzii* and are often found growing nearby. It is important for all seekers of hallucinogenic mushrooms to be aware of the galerinas to avoid poisoning themselves.

Microscopic characters: Spores 8–11 x 5–6.5 μ. Basidia 4-spored. Cheilocystidia present, but not to the exclusion of the basidia. Pleurocystidia present.

» *G. marginata* (FRIES) KUHNER

Cap: 2.5–4(5) cm broad. Convex at first, soon expanding to plane in age. Margin markedly striate. 'Honey' colored when moist, hygrophanous, fading to tan in drying, often leaving a dark band along the margin. Surface smooth overall, moist when wet, not distinctly viscid.

Gills: Attachment adnate, thin and crowded. Pallid in immature fruiting bodies, soon becoming more brownish, eventually dark cinnamon brown.

Stem: 3–5(7) cm long by 2–4 mm thick. Equal, tubular. Surface slightly striated longitudinally or fibrillose with a fine whitish sheath of fibrils towards the base. Partial veil cortinate, leaving a distinct annular zone of fibrils soon colored by spores.

Growth habits and habitat: Growing in cespitose clusters in decaying wood or in decaying wood substratum, and in mosses.

Comments: Poisonous. It is best to avoid all species of *Galerina*. The partial veil of this species is more cortinate while the partial veil of *Galerina autumnalis* tends to be more membranous.

Microscopic characters: Spores 7–8 x 4 μ. Basidia 4-spored. Cheilocystidia present.

The Strophariaceae

THE GENUS *NAEMATOLOMA* KARSTEN

The genus *Naematoloma* is not known for an abundance of distinguishing features. They are typically terrestrial or lignicolous in their habitats and are often found in gregarious groups or in cespitose clusters. Most naematolomas are brightly colored in yellows, oranges, or reds and usually lack a thick gelatinous pellicle on the surface of the cap that is so typical of many psilocybes and strophareas. Taxonomically they are closely related to the psilocybes and are clearly distinguished from them by the presence of microscopic *chrysocystidia*, sterile cells on the gill surface or margin which are highly refractive in tissue revived in 2½% KOH (potassium hydroxide). Only one *Naematoloma* is considered dangerous, *Naematoloma fasciculare*, and fortunately it is not severely poisonous. *Naematoloma popperianum* has been reported to be a producer of psilocybin and/or psilocin though more collections of this species need to be made and studied for authentication. Some pholiotas are very similar to naematolomas, but have rust brown spore deposits and often have fibrillose scales on the caps.

» *N. aurantiaca* (COOKE) GUZMÁN

Cap: 1–4 cm broad (measurements reportedly taken from dried material). Convex to nearly plane with a slight or distinct umbo. Margin even, and striate when moist; often with small whitish veil remnants adhering to it. Scarlet reddish to reddish-brown to rust-reddish and darker at the umbo. Surface smooth and viscid when wet.

Gills: Attachment sinuate to adnate. Whitish at first, soon grayish brown and finally violet at spore maturity, with the edges remaining pallid.

Stem: 3–6.5 cm long by 1.5 mm thick (also taken from dried material). Equal to slightly enlarged at the base. Yellowish overall though more reddish towards the base. Flesh nearly concolorous with peripheral regions of the cap. Partial veil thinly membranous but well-developed, leaving a fragile membranous annulus which soon deteriorates to a distinct annular zone of fibrils on the stem. Whitish to yellowish rhizomorphs present around the base.

Growth habit and habitat: Gregarious to cespitose in soil rich in lignin, on rotten logs, amongst debris in deciduous and coniferous forests in the fall. Reported from California.

Comments: Edibility is undocumented. Formerly placed in *Stropharia*. See also *Psilocybe squamosa*, *Psilocybe thrausta*, and *Naematoloma sublateritium*.

Microscopic characters: Spores (9)10–14(15) x 6–8.5(9.5) μ. Basidia 2- and 4-spored. Pleurocystidia (chrysocystidia) present. Cheilocystidia present causing gill edge to be heteromorphic.

» *N. capnoides* (FRIES) KARSTEN

Cap: 2–7 cm broad. Obtuse to convex with an incurved margin soon expanding to broadly convex to almost flattened, occasionally possessing an obtuse umbo. Margin appendiculate with fine fibrillose remnants of the partial veil, soon disappearing, pale yellowish becoming buff yellow in age. Orange-yellow to orangish cinnamon to yellowish brown with maturity. Surface moist to lubricous, waxy, with buff fibrils but soon becoming smooth. Flesh relatively thick, pallid to whitish.

Gills: Attachment adnate but soon seceding, close, moderately broad to narrow, edges even, and with two or three tiers of intermediate gills. Color white to grayish white when young, then becoming grayish to smoky grayish purple-brown in age.

Stem: 5–9 cm long by 4–10 mm thick. Equal to slightly enlarged at the base, becoming tubular in age. Whitish towards the apex, and pallid to dark tan or rusty brown towards the base. Basal surface covered by scattered fibrils. Partial veil cortinate, leaving a faint superior zone of fibrils.

Growth habit and habitat: Densely gregarious or in large cespitose clusters on conifer wood in the fall, throughout the entire western United States.

Comments: Taste mild and considered edible and good by some. See also *N. fasciculare, N. sublateritium,* and *N. subochraceum.*

Microscopic characters: Spores 6–7 x 4–4.5 μ. Basidia 4-spored. Pleurocystidia (chrysocystidia) present. Cheilocystidia present.

» *N. dispersum* var. *typica*
(FRIES) KARSTEN

Cap: 1–4 cm broad. Conic to convex to broadly convex-umbonate in age. Margin appendiculate from remnants of the partial veil, faintly silky, yellowish to sordid olive and not translucent-striate. Grayish yellow-brown to orange tawny brown at the disc. Surface smooth, lubricous when moist, slightly viscid when very wet. Flesh thin, dingy white to olive.

Gills: Attachment mostly adnate, close, broad. Color whitish when young, then sordid olive and eventually purplish brown with whitish edges.

Stem: 6–10 cm long by 2–5 mm thick. Equal, dry, brittle to pliant in older carpophores (fruiting bodies). Surface densely silky to pruinose near the apex and stiff 'hairs' present about the base. Appressed white fibrillose zones present upon a darkened reddish brown to soot brown stem. Partial veil cortinate, leaving a superior nonpersistent annular zone of fibrils.

Growth habit and habitat: Scattered to gregarious on wood chips and on decayed conifer substratum. Found in the fall to early winter throughout the Pacific Northwest, Idaho, and northern California.

Comments: Taste slightly bitter and unpleasant. Edibility unknown. This species is also called *Hypholoma marginatum* (Pers. ex Fr.) Schroet. See *N. dispersum* var. *idahoense, N. udum,* and *Psilocybe washingtonensis.*

Microscopic characters: Spores 7–9 x 4–5 μ. Basidia 4-spored. Pleurocystidia (chrysocystidia) present. Cheilocystidia present.

» *N. dispersum* var. *idahoense* SMITH

Cap: 1–2.5 cm broad. Obtusely conic becoming campanulate to broadly convex with a small conic umbo. Margin incurved at first and appendiculate with fine web-like remnants of the partial veil. Dull tawny to cinnamon brown, paler towards the edge. Flesh thin, pallid.

Gills: Attachment adnate or adnexed, close narrow to moderately broad. Color whitish becoming sordid grayish brown with edges remaining whitish.

Stem: 6–8 cm long by 1–2 mm thick. Equal, brittle. Sordid brown, gradually darkening from the base upwards. Surface covered by whitish fibrils and lending the appearance of being whitish to the stem at first. Stiff hairs present about the base. Partial veil thin, evanescent.

Growth habit and habitat: Cespitose to subcespitose on conifer logs in the mountains. Found in the fall to early winter in Idaho and possibly from Washington.

Comments: Distinguished from *N. dispersum* var. *typica* by its growth habit. The taste is distinctly bitter. This variety occurs throughout the Pacific Northwest. See also *N. squalidellum.*

Microscopic characters: Spores 7–8.5 x 3.5–4 μ. Basidia 4-spored. Pleurocystidia (chrysocystidia) present. Cheilocystidia present.

» *N. elongatum*
(PERSOON EX FRIES) KONRAD

Cap: .6–2.0 cm broad. Convex becoming broadly convex to nearly plane in age. Margin faintly fringed with fibrils. Deep yellow fading to pale yellow and slightly olivaceous in age. Hygrophanous. Surface moist and smooth. Flesh thin, pale yellow.

Gills: Attachment adnate, subdistant, and broad. Color whitish to pallid yellowish to sordid brown in age.

Stem: 4–10 cm long by 1.5–2.5 mm thick. Equal, tubular, and slightly flexuous or undulated. Pallid becoming yellowish with maturity. Surface silky towards the apex and fibrillose towards the base from the remnants of a thin partial veil.

Growth habit and habitat: Scattered to gregarious in sphagnum bogs. Reported from Washington to California and in the eastern United States in the fall to early winter.

Comments: Taste and odor not distinctive. Spore deposit cinnamon brown. See also *Psilocybe corneipes, N. udum.*

Microscopic characters: Spores (8) 9–11 (12) x 5–6 (7) μ. Basidia 4-spored. Pleurocystidia (chrysocystidia) present. Cheilocystidia present.

» *N. ericaeum* (PERSOON EX FRIES) SMITH

Cap: 1.5–3 (5) cm broad. Conic to conic-campanulate, expanding to convex and then nearly plane. From above, ovoid to ellipsoid at first. Usually with a conic umbo in the younger carpophores (fruiting bodies) but often absent as the cap expands. Margin initially appressed against the stem and at times decorated with whitish veil remnants. Buffy brown to tawny and more olive brown towards the margin. Hygrophanous. Surface smooth, viscid to subviscid when moist from a gelatinous pellicle that is sometimes separable, soon dry. Flesh pale yellowish to pale whitish.

Gills: Attachment adnate becoming sinuate to adnexed and at times seceding, moderately close to subdistant, broad, and slightly enlarged in the center. Color pallid to grayish at first, becoming deep purplish gray to almost black with the edges remaining pallid.

Stem: 4–8 (13) cm long by 2.5–4 (10) mm thick. Subequal to curved at the base. Buff brown overall. Surface covered with pallid fibrils towards the apex. Partial veil cortinate, fugacious, leaving annular zone of fibrils soon darkened with spores.

Growth habit and habitat: Scattered to gregarious on grassy wet soil near ponds and in low damp areas in open pine woods. Suspected to grow throughout the Pacific Northwest, and officially reported from California, Tennessee, Alabama, Michigan, and Ohio.

Comments: A very rare species. *N. ericaeum* was also known as *Stropharia subumbonatescens* Murrill and *Psilocybe ericaea* Quélet. More work needs to be done with this species to resolve some confusing taxonomic problems. See also *Psilocybe stuntzii* (field variety), *Psilocybe semilanceata,* and *Psilocybe californica.*

Microscopic characters: Spores 11–13.5 x 6.5–8 μ. Basidia 4-spored. Pleurocystidia (chrysocystidia) present. Cheilocystidia present.

» *N. fasciculare* (FRIES) KARSTEN

Cap: 1–8 cm broad, usually 2–5 cm broad when in large colonies. Obtusely conic becoming campanulate, expanding to broadly convex-umbonate or nearly plane. Margin incurved and appendiculate at first. Yellowish orange-brown to greenish yellow. Surface lubricous when moist, mostly smooth but at times minutely silky towards the margin which is often tinged greenish. Flesh moderately thick and yellowish towards the disc, staining sordid brown where cut.

Gills: Attachment adnate, sometimes seceding, crowed, narrow, with several tiers of intermediate gills. Color pallid sulphur yellow becoming olivaceous or greenish yellow in age.

Stem: 5–12 cm long by 3–10 mm thick. Tapering more narrowly towards the base, often wavy and contorted, and hollow. Sulphur yellow at first but soon becoming tawny to rusty brown from the base upwards. Surface appressed fibrillose below the annular zone, and smooth above. Flesh yellowish. Partial veil thin, leaving an evanescent fibrillose annular zone in the superior region of the stem.

Growth habit and habitat: Usually in cespitose clusters, growing on hardwood and conifer stumps and logs in the fall, or in decayed conifer substratum early winter and spring throughout the Pacific Northwest and California.

Comments: Very bitter in its taste. Gastrointestinally poisonous, and in severe cases may cause death. The greenish tint to the gills, its typical cespitose habit on decaying wood, and the color of the cap are the most characteristic features of this species. See also *N. capnoides.*

Microscopic characters: Spores 6.5–8 x 3.5–4 μ. Basidia 4-spored. Pleurocystidia (chrysocystidia) present. Cheilocystidia present.

» *N. olivaceotinctum* (KAUFFMAN) SMITH

Cap: 1.5–3 cm broad. Obtusely campanulate expanding to plane, with an incurved margin at first. Dull greenish to olive, often becoming pinkish buff. Flesh thin and mostly concolorous with the cap, fragile. Surface moist, smooth, and faintly translucent-striate along the margin.

Gills: Attachment adnate, close to subdistant, thin to moderately broad. Color pale olive-gray then dingy yellowish brown.

Stem: 3–5 cm long by 1.5–2.5 mm thick. Equal to narrowing downwards, smooth, brittle, and tubular. Color bright reddish brown towards apex while more chestnut brown toward the base.

Growth habit and habitat: Gregarious to scattered on rich humus or on debris from the outwashes of streams in conifer forests in the fall to early winter. Found in Washington, Oregon, California, and reported from New York.

Comments: This mushroom usually can be distinguished from other species of this genus by the greenish color of the cap. However, to a degree, this characteristic is shared in drying by *N. polytrichi, N. squalidellum,* and *N. udum.*

Microscopic characters: Spores 9–12 x 4.5–5.5 (6) μ. Basidia 4-spored. Pleurocystidia (chrysocystidia) present. Cheilocystidia present.

» *N. polytrichi* (FRIES) KONRAD

Cap: 1–2.5 cm broad. Obtusely conic to campanulate and finally expanding to convex and often with a low umbo. Having a translucent-striate margin when moist, sometimes finely appendiculate along the edge. Dingy pale tawny to olivaceous brown, fading to pale yellow. Surface subviscid when moist. Flesh yellowish and brittle.

Gills: Attachment adnate, close, narrow. Color greenish yellow at first, becoming dark sordid purplish brown.

Stem: 5–7 long by 1.5–2.5 mm thick. Equal, very brittle, and smooth with faint fibrillose patches below and pruinose above. Color tawny brown to sordid towards the base and pale greenish yellow near the apex.

Growth habit and habitat: Gregarious in the fall in mossy soil near bogs. Found in Washington and probably elsewhere in the Pacific Northwest. Also known from Michigan and New Hampshire.

Comments: This species has essentially the same overall appearance as *N. squalidellum* and *N. udum.*

Microscopic characters: Spores 7–9 x 3.5–4(4.5) μ. Basidia 4-spored. Pleurocystidia (chrysocystidia) present. Cheilocystidia present.

» *N. popperianum* SINGER

Cap: About 3 cm broad. Convex with an incurved margin, expanding to broadly convex with the margin remaining slightly incurved. Yellowish tan with faint brownish areas, surface smooth and viscid when moist.

Gills: Attachment adnate, close, broad. Color deep orangish brown.

Stem: 2.5 cm long by 4–5 mm thick. Equal to slightly enlarged in the center. Whitish to pallid. Surface above annulus smooth, while below covered with whitish tufts of the partial veil. Partial veil membranous, leaving a superior membranous annulus. Context whitish or bluing where bruised. White rhizomorphs present around the base of the stem.

Growth habit and habitat: Solitary. One collection was found in the San Francisco Bay Area on a rubbish heap near woods.

Comments: Thought to contain psilocin or psilocybin. It has been placed in this genus because of the nature and abundance of chrysocystidia, sterile cells on the surface of the gills which have certain highly refractive properties in tissue revived in 2½% KOH (potassium hydroxide). This is the first species of *Naematoloma* known to bruise bluish green. See also *Psilocybe sp.* and *Psilocybe stuntzii.*

Microscopic characters: Spores (9) 10–14 (15) x 6–8.5 (10) μ. Basidia 2- and 4-spored. Pleurocystidia (chrysocystidia) present. Cheilocystidia present, causing the gill edge to be heteromorphic.

» *N. squalidellum* (PECK) SMITH

Cap: 1–3 (4) cm broad. Conic to convex to campanulate to broadly convex or plane with an obtuse umbo. Margin appendiculate, faintly striate, and often recurved in umbonate carpophores. Bright or sordid rusty brown when moist, fading to yellowish buff. Surface smooth and not viscid when moist.

Gills: Attachment adnate and occasionally uncinate, close, narrow to broad in extreme age. Color pale greenish yellow becoming purple-brown with spore maturity.

Stem: 3–5 cm long (in peat) or 6–10 cm long (in moss) by 1.5–3.0 mm thick. Equal and very brittle. Surface covered at first with patches of appressed fibrils from the rudimentary partial veil. Pallid brownish towards the base at first, then rusty brown and finally sordid blackish brown below while pale olivaceous to pale yellowish above.

Growth habit and habitat: Cespitose to gregarious or scattered on humus near bogs or on peaty soil or on debris left from high waters of streams in the fall. Found in the Olympic Peninsula in Washington, probably elsewhere in the Pacific Northwest and also in the Northeastern United States.

Comments: Generally resembling *N. udum* and *N. polytrichi.*

Microscopic characters: Spores (8) 9–11 (12) x (4) 5–6 μ. Basidia 4-spored. Pleurocystidia (chrysocystidia) present. Cheilocystidia present.

» *N. sublateritium* (FRIES) KARSTEN

Cap: 2–8 (10) cm broad. Convex to broadly convex, soon becoming plane and occasionally with a broad umbo. Margin incurved at first, and appendiculate with fibrillose remnants of the cortinate partial veil. Yellowish near the margin and more orange-red to reddish brown towards the disc. Surface only moist when wet, covered with appressed fibrils and almost scaly near the margin in fresh fruiting bodies. Flesh relatively thick, pallid brownish and often bruising yellowish.

Gills: Attachment adnate and soon seceding, close, broad, and with 3–5 tiers of intermediate gills. Yellowish to olivaceous at first, soon becoming grayish to dark purple gray at spore maturity.

Stem: 5–9 cm long by 5–10 mm thick. Equal overall and solid. Pallid to whitish, soon bruising yellowish, and becoming rust brown from the base. Surface almost scaly at the base, covered with appressed fibrils below the annular zone, and pruinose above. Partial veil cortinate, leaving an annular zone of fibrils darkened by spores.

Growth habit and habitat: Subcespitose to cespitose on rotting hardwood logs or stumps, especially oak. Found throughout Eastern and Central United States in the fall. Very rarely occurring in the west.

Comments: Considered edible and good by many. The reddish color of the cap, especially at the disc, is a distinguishing feature of this mushroom. See also *N. aurantiaca* and *N. capnoides.*

Microscopic characters: Spores 6–7.5 x 3.5–4 μ. Basidia 4-spored. Pleurocystidia (chrysocystidia) present. Cheilocystidia present.

» *N. subochraceum* SMITH

Cap: 2–4 cm broad. Convex at first with an inrolled margin, expanding with age to broadly convex and eventually plane. Margin sometimes decorated with fine fibrillose remnants of the partial veil, soon disappearing. Pale ochraceous-tawny overall, though tending to be more yellowish along the margin. Surface extremely viscid to glutinous when moist from a separable gelatinous pellicle. Flesh thin, relatively firm, and yellowish in coloration.

Gills: Attachment adnate to subdecurrent, close, and thin to moderately broad. Generally two tiers of intermediate gills present. Pale yellow in youngest stages of development, soon becoming sordid cinnamon brown with maturity.

Stem: 5–9 cm long by 5–7 mm thick. Equal to enlarged at the base or apex. Surface in lower two thirds covered by a sheath of fine yellowish to whitish fibrils. Partial veil cortinate, usually leaving a fragile annular zone of fibrils soon becoming darkened by spores. Yellowish towards the apex, becoming sordid rusty brown from the base upwards in age.

Growth habit and habitat: Gregarious to cespitose on decaying conifer logs and stumps in the fall. Known from the Olympics, the Cascades of Washington and Oregon, extending well into northern California.

Comments: Edibility is undocumented. The viscidity and coloration of the cap are two very distinctive features of this species. See also *N. capnoides.*

Microscopic characters: Spores 5–6 x 2.5–3.0 μ. Basidia 4-spored. Pleurocystidia (chrysocystidia) and cheilocystidia present.

» *N. udum* (PERSOON EX FRIES) KARSTEN

Cap: 1–3 cm broad. Obtusely conic to convex at first, becoming broadly convex or plane in age, and at times barely umbonate. Margin often slightly incurved. Color variable, from pale to dark rusty brown to yellowish brown and finally pale yellow or buff. If watersoaked, may be dark purplish brown and tinged olive in places. Surface smooth, and lubricous when wet. Flesh thickest at the disc, yellowish and pliant.

Gills: Attachment adnate, close to subdistant, broad. Color whitish to pale yellowish at first, then sordid purplish brown with olive-yellowish tints, while the edges remain whitish.

Stem: 4–12 cm long by 1.5–4 mm thick. Equal, tubular, and brittle. Surface covered with scattered patches of appressed fibrils from the rudimentary partial veil. Dark rusty brown below and pale yellowish or at times whitish above.

Growth habit and habitat: Scattered to gregarious in wet humus near sphagnum bogs in conifer woods in the fall. Found in the eastern United States; suspected to occur in the Pacific Northwest.

Comments: Edibility not documented. Similar in appearance to *N. elongatum*, differing macroscopically in the color of spore deposit, which is purplish brown.

Microscopic characters: Spores slightly marbled, 14–18(20) x 5–7 μ. Basidia 4-spored. Pleurocystidia (chrysocystidia) present. Cheilocystidia present, causing the gill edge to be heteromorphic.

THE GENUS *PSILOCYBE* KUMMER

In the Strophariaceae, *Psilocybe* is strikingly similar to *Naematoloma* and *Stropharia*, and is separated from these two genera with difficulty when solely using macroscopic features. *Psilocybe* can be found in a wide range of habitats: in dung, moss, soil, or in decayed wood. Many species have viscid deep brown caps when moist that fade in drying to brown, and most but not all hallucinogenic species bruise bluish green. *Psilocybe* lacks the *chrysocystidia* cells of *Naematoloma* and *Stropharia*, though other types of microscopic sterile cells on the gill can be present. Often, a species which had been originally described as a *Stropharia* by one mycologist will be later classified as a *Psilocybe* by another. These taxonomic concepts will continue to change as a new definition of the genus *Psilocybe* evolves.

» *P. angustispora* SMITH

Cap: 2–6 mm broad. Acutely conic to conic-campanulate. Margin decorated at first with white fibrillose remnants of the veil. Dark reddish brown when moist, fading to pale pinkish tan in drying. Surface smooth and viscid from a thick gelatinous separable pellicle. Flesh very thin and pliant.

Gills: Attachment subdecurrent, distant to subdistant, broad. Becoming dark purple-brown in age with the edges whitish fringed.

Stem: 1.0–2.0 cm long by .5 mm thick. Equal. Pallid pinkish tan or nearly concolorous with the cap. Surface covered with pallid fibrils and the lower portions often with minute fibrillose scales. Partial veil thin, cortinate.

Growth habit and habitat: Single to several on the dung of sheep or wild animals such as elk or marmot during the spring and fall. Reported from Washington and probably to be found elsewhere in the Pacific Northwest.

Comments: Not known to be hallucinogenic. See also *P. coprophila* and *P. semilanceata*.

Microscopic characters: Spores 12–15 x 5–6 μ. Basidia 4-spored. Pleurocystidia absent. Cheilocystidia present.

» *P. baeocystis* SINGER AND SMITH

Cap: 1.5–5.5 cm broad. Conic to obtusely conic to convex, expanding to plane only in extreme age. Margin incurved at first, and distinctly undulated when convex; translucent-striate and often tinted greenish. Dark olive-brown to buff brown (occasionally steel blue), becoming copper brown in the center when drying. Hygrophanous. Soon bruising bluish green. Surface viscid when moist from a gelatinous pellicle, usually separable.

Gills: Attachment adnate to uncinate, subclose. Color grayish to dark cinnamon brown with the edges remaining pallid.

Stem: 5–7 cm long by 2–3 mm thick. Equal to subequal. Pallid to brownish surface sometimes covered with fine whitish fibrils while often more yellowish towards the apex. Brittle, stuffed with loose fibers. Distinct rhizomorphs present about stem base. Partial veil thinly cortinate, rapidly becoming inconspicuous.

Growth habit and habitat: Solitary to gregarious to subcespitose on decaying conifer mulch, in wood chips, or in lawns with high lignin content. Found in the fall to early winter and to a lesser degree in the spring. (I have found it as late as June 20.) First reported from Oregon, common in Washington, British Columbia, and elsewhere in the Pacific Northwest.

Comments: Contains psilocybin and/or psilocin. Very potent. See *P. caerulipes, P. strictipes, P. caerulescens,* and *P. cyanescens.*

Microscopic characters: Spores 10–12 x 6–7 μ. Basidia 4-spored. Pleurocystidia absent. Cheilocystidia present causing gill edge to be heteromorphic.

» *P. caerulescens* MURRILL

Cap: 2–9 cm broad. Obtusely campanulate to convex with a decurved margin at first, becoming convex, rarely plane in extreme age and often having either a small umbo or a slight depression in the center. Margin often bluish, translucent-striate halfway to the center portion of the cap and hanging with fragile whitish veil remnants (appendiculate). Deep olive-black in young specimens, hygrophanous, fading with age to a dark reddish brown to chestnut brown near the disc and often darker towards the margins. Surface smooth and slightly viscid to lubricous when moist, pellicle thinly gelatinous but not usually separable. Flesh whitish to dingy brown, moderately thick, and bruising bluish green.

Gills: Attachment sinuate to adnate, close to subclose, and broad. Color grayish to 'soot' brown with the edges remaining whitish.

Stem: 4–12 cm long by 2–10 mm thick. Mostly equal but often radicating into a long pseudorhiza. Covered at first with a whitish layer of fibrils which soon deteriorates revealing a more sordid brown smooth surface underneath. Partial veil cortinate, whitish and copious at first, but soon disappearing. Flesh stuffed and fibrous; bruising bluish green, whitish rhizomorphs (bluish when disturbed) present about the base of the stem.

Growth habit and habitat: Gregarious to cespitose in the late spring and summer. First reported from Alabama. Suspected to occur elsewhere in the southeastern United States, common in Mexico. Inhabiting soil or sugar cane mulch, in disturbed or cultivated soils.

Comments: Contains psilocybin and/or psilocin. Very bitter in taste.

Microscopic characters: Spores 6–8 x 4–6 μ. Basidia 4-spored, occasionally 2-spored. Pleurocystidia absent. Cheilocystidia present.

» *P. caerulipes* (PECK) SACCARDO

Cap: 1.0–3.5 cm broad. Obtusely conic becoming conic-campanulate to broadly convex to plane with age and may retain a slight umbo. Margin incurved at first, often tinged greenish, very irregular, and closely translucent-striate. Cinnamon brown to dingy brown, hygrophanous, fading to pale ocharaceous buff. Surface viscid when moist from a gelatinous pellicle, but soon becoming dry and shiny. Flesh thin, pliant, and bluing where bruised.

Gills: Attachment adnate to uncinate, close to crowded, narrow, with edges remaining whitish. Color sordid brown at first becoming rusty cinnamon.

Stem: 3–6 cm long by 2–3 mm thick. Equal to slightly enlarged toward the base. White to buff at first, with the lower regions dingy brown at maturity, bluing where bruised. Surface powdered at the apex, and covered with whitish to grayish fibrils downwards. Flesh stuffed with a pith and solid at first but soon becoming tubular. Partial veil thin, cortinate, and forming an evanescent fibrillose annular zone in the superior region of the stem if at all.

Growth habit and habitat: Solitary to cespitose on hardwood debris and on or about decaying hardwood logs, particularly birch and maple. Growing in the summer to early fall after warm rains. Widely distributed throughout the Midwestern and eastern United States, from Maine to North Carolina to Tennessee to Michigan.

Comments: Contains psilocin and psilocybin. The bluing reaction may take a few hours to express itself. See also *P. baeocystis.*

Microscopic characters: Spores 7–10 x 4.5–5 μ from 4-spored basidia. Spores from 2-spored basidia are larger. Pleurocystidia absent. Cheilocystidia present causing the gill edge to be heteromorphic.

» *P. californica* EARLE

Cap: 1–3 cm broad. Obtusely conic to convex at first, expanding to broadly convex to plane with age. Margin often adorned with whitish fibrils and translucent-striate when moist halfway to disc. Chestnut brown to very dark dull brownish, hygrophanous (fading in drying) from the center of the cap. Surface smooth, viscid when moist from a thin gelatinous pellicle. Flesh thin, paler than the color of the cap.

Gills: Attachment adnate, close to crowded, and moderately broad. Pallid to pale brownish at first, becoming purple-brown with spore maturity.

Stem: 2–6 cm long by 1–2 mm thick. Equal and flexuous. Brownish to pale reddish brown. Surface slightly silky (fibrillose). Context stuffed with a whitish pith and soon becoming hollow.

Growth habit and habitat: Growing in gregarious to subcespitose clusters in grassy areas and beside roads in the spring and fall. Reported from California and New York.

Comments: Not known to be hallucinogenic. See also *Naematoloma ericaeum* and *Psilocybe subviscida.*

Microscopic characters: Spores 6–7 x 3.5–4 μ. Basidia 4-spored. Pleurocystidia absent. Cheilocystidia present.

» *P. coprophila*
(BULLIARD EX FRIES) KUMMER

Cap: 1–3 cm broad. Convex or hemispheric. Margin sometimes finely appendiculate, usually translucent-striate halfway to disc. Orangish brown to reddish brown. Hygrophanous. Surface viscid when moist from a separable gelatinous pellicle; smooth overall

with buff fibrils along the margin. Flesh relatively thin and nearly concolorous with the cap.

Gills: Attachment adnate, broad, and subdistant. Color grayish brown at first, then deep purple brown to black with spore maturity.

Stem: 2–6 cm long by 1–3 mm thick. Nearly equal. Yellow to yellowish brown. Surface covered with scattered fibrils and dry. Partial veil thin to absent. Sometimes bruising bluish in the mycelium.

Growth habit and habitat: Usually found on cow or horse dung in the spring, summer, and fall. Never cespitose but scattered to numerous. Widely distributed across the continent.

Comments: This mushroom readily fades upon drying, and the margin loses its translucent-striate appearance. Some strains have been reported to be hallucinogenic, though weakly so. See also *P. angustispora, P. subviscida* and *P. merdaria.*

Microscopic characters: Spores 11–15 x 6.5–9 μ. Pleurocystidia absent. Cheilocystidia present.

» *P. corneipes*
(FRIES) KARSTEN, HATTSVAMPAR

Cap: 1–3 cm broad. Obtusely conic with an inrolled margin in young fruiting bodies, expanding to campanulate or broadly convex, and can be umbonate with a broad or conic umbo. Margin translucent-striate, particularly seen with age. Dull to bright orange or orange brown. Surface glabrous and shiny. Flesh thickest at the disc and thinning towards the margin, firm, pale yellowish to tawny.

Gills: Attachment adnate to seceding, broad, and close. Color pallid to pale buff and finally grayish brown.

Stem: 3–5 cm long by 1.5–2.0 mm thick. Yellowish to pale orange or dull tawny towards the apex, dark reddish brown below, and blackening from the base upwards. Surface smooth, slightly powdered above. Coarse stiff 'hairs' or fibrils may be present at the base. Flesh brittle and hollow.

Growth habit and habitat: Scattered to gregarious in moss along the edges of high sphagnum bogs in the mountains in late spring, summer, and fall. Throughout western United States and Canada.

Comments: Edibility is unknown. See also *Naematoloma udum* and *Naematoloma elongatum.* This species resembles some galerinas.

Microscopic characters: Spores rough, 6–7.5 x 4–5 μ. Basidia 4-spored. Pleurocystidia present. Cheilocystidia present.

» *P. cubensis* (EARLE) SINGER

Cap: 1.5–8.0 cm broad. Conic-campanulate often with an acute umbo at first, becoming convex to broadly convex and finally plane in age with or without an obtuse or acute umbo. Reddish cinnamon brown in young fruiting bodies, becoming lighter with age to a more yellowish brown, fading to pale yellow or white at the margins with the umbo or center region remaining more cinnamon brown. Surface viscid to lubricous when moist but soon dry; universal veil leaving remnants on cap but soon becoming smooth overall. Flesh whitish, soon bruising bluish.

Gills: Attachment adnate to adnexed, soon seceding, close, narrow to slightly enlarged in the center. Pallid to grayish in young fruiting bodies, becoming deep purplish gray to nearly black in maturity, often mottled.

Stem: 4–15 cm long by 5–15 mm thick. Thickening towards the base in most specimens. Whitish overall but may discolor to yellowish; bruising bluish green where injured. Surface smooth to striated at the apex, and dry. Partial veil membranous, leaving a persistent membranous annulus.

Growth habit and habitat: Scattered to gregarious on dung of cows and horses or on well manured grounds in the spring, summer, and fall. Found throughout the southeastern United States.

Comments: This species is easy to recognize by its size, the membranous annulus, the blue-staining stem, and the habitat. It is the most widely cultivated of hallucinogenic mushrooms, and for this reason some strains may adapt to other regions of North America. See also *P. sp.* and *Naematoloma popperianum.*

Microscopic characters: Spores 11.5–17 x 8–11 μ. Basidia 2-3-4-spored. Pleurocystidia present. Cheilocystidia present.

» *P. cyanescens* WAKEFIELD

Cap: 2–4 cm broad. Obtusely conic to conic-convex at first, usually soon expanding to broadly convex to nearly plane in age with an undulating or wavy margin. Margin translucent-striate. Chestnut brown in young specimens, becoming more 'carmel' colored with age, hygrophanous, fading to yellowish brown or ochraceous in drying. Surface smooth and viscid when moist from a separable gelatinous pellicle. Context nearly concolorous with the cap and bruising bluish green.

Gills: Attachment adnate to subdecurrent, close to subdistant, broad. Color cinnamon brown becoming deep smoky brown with the edges remaining paler.

Stem: 6–8 cm long by 2.5–5.0 mm thick. Often curved and somewhat enlarged at the base, stiff not pliant. Whitish overall, readily bruising bluish. Surface silky, covered with fine fibrils and often with long whitish rhizomorphs protruding about base of stem. Partial veil copiously cortinate, snow-white, rapidly deteriorating to an obscure annular zone if at all.

Growth habit and habitat: Scattered to gregarious in humus enriched with lignin amongst leaves and twigs, in wood chips, or in well decayed conifer substratum. Often under douglas fir or cedar and in heavily mulched rhododendron beds. Found in the fall to early winter in the Pacific Northwest. Reported from Washington, Oregon, California and British Columbia.

Comments: Very potent. Contains psilocybin and/or psilocin. The color of the cap and the copious nature of the partial veil are very distinctive of this species. See also *P. strictipes* and *P. baeocystis.*

· **Microscopic characters:** Spores 9–12 x 5–8 μ. Basidia 4-spored. Pleurocystidia present. Cheilocystidia present, causing the edge to be heteromorphic.

» *P. merdaria* (FRIES) RICKEN

Cap: 1–4 cm broad. Campanulate-hemispheric to convex to broadly convex, and sometimes slightly umbonate, finally expanding to plane with age. Margin translucent-striate when moist and often appendiculate with remnants of the thin partial veil. Near cinnamon brown to livid brown when moist, fading to ochraceous or yellowish brown, and remaining darker at the disc. Surface smooth and only moist to subviscid when wet.

Gills: Attachment adnate to subdecurrent, close to broad. Yellowish at first, darkening with spore maturity to a dark brown.

Stem: 2–4 (+) cm long by 1–3 mm thick. Pale yellowish to pallid. Surface covered by fine fibrils and dry. Flesh stuffed with a fibrous pith, tough, but soon becoming hollow. Partial veil thinly membranous, fugacious, soon deteriorating to an annular zone of fibrils in the median to lower regions of the stem, usually darkened by spores.

Growth habit and habitat: Scattered to numerous on dung. Reported from California, Oregon, Washington, and the north central midwest. It is likely that this species is more widespread than the literature presently indicates.

Comments: Some varieties may be weakly hallucinogenic. See also *Psilocybe coprophila* and *Psilocybe subviscida.*

Microscopic characters: Spores 12–17 x 7–8 μ. Basidia 4-spored. Pleurocystidia absent. Cheilocystidia not observed.

» *P. montana*   (FRIES) QUELET

Cap: 0.5–2.0 cm broad. Obtusely conic at first but rapidly expanding to convex to broadly convex and may be slightly umbonate. Margin translucent-striate when moist. Dark reddish brown, hygrophanous, fading to light yellowish brown to grayish brown in drying. Surface smooth, not distinctly viscid when wet.

Gills: Attachment adnate, subdistant, thin to moderately broad. Color light brownish to very dark reddish brown with spore maturity.

Stem: 2–4 cm long by 1–2 mm thick. Mostly equal to slightly enlarged at the base and usually flexuous. Reddish brown overall or nearly concolorous with the cap. Surface dry, smooth or having a few scattered fibrils. Partial veil thin to obscure.

Growth habit and habitat: Scattered to numerous, usually found in moss or in sandy soils and often at high elevations. Reported throughout Western North America and from Michigan.

Comments: Edibility is not documented; presently not known to be hallucinogenic. Also known as *P. atrorufa. P. bullacea* is now considered synonomous with *P. montana.*

Microscopic characters: Spores 5.5–8 x 4–5 μ. Basidia 4-spored. Pleurocystidia absent. Cheilocystidia present.

» *P. pelliculosa*   (SMITH) SINGER AND SMITH

Cap: 0.5–2(3) cm broad. Obtusely conic becoming conic-campanulate with age. Margin translucent-striate and generally not incurved in young specimens. Chestnut brown when moist, then dark dingy yellow to pale yellow in drying (hygrophanous) often with a pallid band along the margin, and frequently tinged olive-green in patches. Surface smooth, viscid when moist from a separable gelatinous pellicle. Flesh thin, pliant, and more or less concolorous with the cap.

Gills: Attachment adnate to adnexed, finally seceding, close, narrow to moderately broad. Color dull cinnamon brown, darkening with spores in age.

Stem: 6–8 cm long by 1–2.5 mm thick. Equal above, and slightly enlarged at the base. Surface is covered with appressed grayish fibrils, and powdered at the apex. Whitish to pallid to grayish, more brownish toward the base, blue-green where bruised or in age. Flesh stuffed with a tough pith. Partial veil thin to obscure or absent.

Growth habit and habitat: Scattered to gregarious to cespitose on well decayed conifer substratum, in mulch, or in soil rich in lignin. Often seen along paths in coniferous forests. Found in the fall to early winter throughout the Pacific Northwest and in Northern California.

Comments: Hallucinogenic, though weak. There seems to be two varieties of this species, one with a whitish stem and one with a more dingy brown stem. *P. pelliculosa* is nearly identical with *P. silvatica* and is distinguished from it by the length of the spores. See also *P. washingtonensis* and *P. semilanceata.*

Microscopic characters: Spores 9–13 x 5–7 μ. Basidia 4-spored. Pleurocystidia absent. Cheilocystidia present, causing the gill edge to be heteromorphic.

» *P. quebecensis*   OLA'H AND HEIM

Cap: 1–3(3.5) cm broad. Nearly hemispheric at first, soon expanding to convex, then becoming broadly convex to plane, and without an umbo. Margin incurved at first and usually not markedly undulated; translucent-striate when moist. Pale straw yellow and often with brownish or tawny hues, becoming more grayish in drying. Bruising bluish green when touched or disturbed. Surface smooth, becoming finely wrinkled with age, and viscid when moist. Flesh whitish.

Gills: Attachment adnate, thin, moderately broad to swollen in the middle. Becoming very dark chestnut brown at maturity, usually somewhat mottled, with the edges remaining whitish.

Stem: 2–3.5(4.5) cm long by 1–2(2.5) mm thick. Slightly enlarged at the apex and flared at the base which is often furnished with rhizomorphs, brittle, tough, and fibrous. Yellowish tawny, drying to a distinct grayish yellow, becoming bluish green where bruised. Partial veil cortinate, fugacious, and soon disappearing.

Growth habit and habitat: Growing in sandy soils, particularly in outwashes of streams, and growing in decayed wood substratum of alder, birch, fir, and spruce in the late summer and fall. Reported from Quebec, specifically in the Jacques Carter river region.

Comments: Hallucinogenic. See also *P. baeocystis* and *P. caerulipes*.

Microscopic characters: Spores 6–8 x 9–11 μ. Basidia 4-spored. Pleurocystidia present, 12–30(35) x 9–15 μ, very distinctive by their swollen apices, as in *Psilocybe cubensis* and *Psilocybe cyanescens*. Cheilocystidia present, causing the gill edge to be heteromorphic.

» *P. semilanceata* (FRIES) KUMMER

Cap: .5–2.5 cm broad. Conic to obtusely conic to conic-campanulate with an acute umbo. Margin translucent-striate, incurved and sometimes undulated in young fruiting bodies, often darkened by spores. Color variable, extremely hygrophanous. Usually dark chestnut brown when moist, soon drying to a light tan or yellowish and occasionally with an olive tint. Surface viscid when moist from a separable gelatinous pellicle.

Gills: Attachment mostly adnexed, close to crowded, narrow. Color pallid at first, rapidly becoming brownish and finally purplish brown with the edges remaining pallid.

Stem: 4–10 cm long by .75–2(3) mm thick. Slender, equal, flexuous, and pliant. Pallid to more brownish towards the base. Surface smooth overall. Context stuffed with a fibrous pith. Partial veil thinly cortinate, rapidly deteriorating, leaving an obscure evanescent

annular zone of fibrils, usually darkened by spores. Often, this zone is entirely absent.

Growth habit and habitat: Scattered to gregarious in pastures and in fields or in other grassy areas. Especially abundant in or about sedge clumps grass in the more damp parts of the fields. Reported throughout the Pacific Northwest west of the Cascades from northern California to British Columbia in the fall to early winter, and to a much lesser degree in the spring along the coastal areas of Oregon and Washington.

Comments: Hallucinogenic. In the northwest this species is one of the most common of active psilocybes and the easiest for amateurs to identify. See also *P. angustispora*, *P. pelliculosa*, and *P. silvatica*.

Microscopic characters: Spores 12–14 x 7–8 μ. Basidia 4-spored. Pleurocystidia absent. Cheilocystidia present, causing gill edge to be heteromorphic.

» *P. silvatica* (PECK) SINGER AND SMITH

Cap: .8–2.5 cm broad. Obtusely conic to campanulate, and often with an acute umbo. Tawny dark brown when moist, fading to pale yellowish brown or grayish brown. Surface smooth, viscid when moist from a thin gelatinous pellicle that is barely separable, if at all.

Gills: Attachment adnate to adnexed, close to subdistant, narrow to moderately broad. Color dull rusty brown at maturity.

Stem: 2–8 cm long by 1–3 mm thick. Equal to slightly enlarged at the base, brittle, tubular, and somewhat flexuous. Pallid to brownish beneath a whitish fribrillose covering. Partial veil poorly developed, cortinate, thin to obscure, and soon absent.

Growth habit and habitat: Gregarious but not cespitose on wood debris or on wood chips or in well decayed conifer substratum in the fall. Known from the eastern United States from Michigan to New York to Ontario and the Pacific Northwest.

Comments: Contains psilocybin and/or psilocin. Not potent for its weight. Differing from *P. pelliculosa* in the length of the spores and cheilocystidia.

Microscopic characters: Spores 6–9.5 x 4.5–5.5 μ from 4-spored basidia; 2-spored basidia present as well. Pleurocystidia absent. Cheilocystidia present, causing the gill edge to be heteromorphic.

» *P. sp.*

Cap: 1.5–4.0 cm broad. Broadly convex to almost plane at maturity. Whitish to more of a smoky brown in the center. Surface smooth, and soon dry. Context whitish and weakly bruising bluish-green.

Gills: Attachment adnate to subdecurrent, close to subdistant, narrow to moderately broad. Color dull grayish brown.

Stem: 3–4 cm long by 1.5–3 mm thick. Equal to slightly enlarged at the base, hollow, and stuffed with a loose whitish pith that weakly bruises blue-green. Overall color pallid. Partial veil membranous, leaving a small but fairly persistent membranous annulus.

Growth habit and habitat: Growing on horse dung. Reported from California.

Comments: See also *P. cubensis* and *N. popperianum*. Apparently hallucinogenic.

Microscopic characters: Spores 7.5–10(11.5) x 6–8 μ. Basidia 2- and 4-spored. Pleurocystidia present. Cheilocystidia present, causing the gill edge to be heteromorphic.

» *P. squamosa* (PERSOON EX FRIES) ORTON

Cap: 3–8 cm broad. Conic or obtusely conic when young with an incurved margin, soon becoming broadly campanulate to convex, and often with a conic umbo. Viscid when moist from a separable gelatinous pellicle, but soon drying. Yellowish brown to orangish brown overall. At first adorned with small scales or 'squamules' along the margin, but soon smooth and free of veil remnants. Flesh relatively thin and watery brown when wet.

Gills: Attachment adnate to uncinate, close to subdistant, moderately broad, with two to three tiers of intermediate gills inserted. Pallid bluish gray, then dark grayish brown to purple brown when fully mature.

Stem: 6–12 cm long by 4–8 mm thick. Equal to slightly enlarged and curved at the base, hollow, and somewhat fragile. Whitish towards the apex and sordid brown to dense buff below the annulus. Surface covered with evanescent pallid to brownish recurved scales, often with orange-buff rhizomorphs protruding about the base. Partial veil membranous, fragile, leaving a superior membranous annulus, striated on the top side, often hanging broken around the stem, or entirely absent in age.

Growth habit and habitat: Solitary to scattered in the late summer and fall in meadows and mixed conifer and alder woods. Known from the Pacific Northwest, Minnesota, and California. It is likely this species is widely distributed across the continent.

Comments: There are conflicting reports on the edibility of *P. squamosa;* caution is definitely recommended. Once a *Stropharia,* this species lacks the chrysocystidia now typical of that genus. Both the squamules of the cap and the annulus are temporal features; however, they are considered taxonomically significant. See *P. thrausta* and *Naematoloma aurantiaca,* which are very similar but differ in the reddish coloration of the caps. *S. hornemannii* resembles this species in a more general sense.

Microscopic characters: Spores 11–15 x 6–8 μ with a central germ pore. Basidia 4-spored. Cheilocystidia present. Pleurocystidia absent.

» *P. strictipes* SINGER AND SMITH

Cap: 2–4(5) cm broad. Convex to campanulate at first, becoming broadly convex with an undulated margin, expanding to plane only in exteme age. Margin translucent-striate when moist in fresh fruiting bodies and usually wavy. Dull yellowish brown to olive-brown when moist, hygrophanous. Surface viscid when moist from a separable gelatinous pellicle. Flesh mostly concolorous with the cap and bruising bluish green.

Gills: Attachment adnate, close, narrow, and with three tiers of intermediate gills. Color pallid in very young fruiting bodies, becoming dark chocolate brown as the spores ripen with the edges remaining whitish.

Stem: 10–13 cm long by 2–3 mm thick. Equal, straight, long, and very brittle. Pallid but readily bruising bluish green. Surface covered with pallid fibrils, and with stiff hairs about the base. Partial veil thin, evanescent, leaving a pseudo-annular zone near the apex which soon disappears.

Growth habit and habitat: Gregarious to subcespitose on decaying conifer debris, amongst twigs and leaves, in soil high in lignin content, and on borders of fields. Reported from Washington and Oregon and may be expected to occur elsewhere in the Pacific

Northwest. Found in the fall to early winter.

Comments: Contains psilocybin and/or psilocin. Distinguished from other psilocybes of this type by the length of the stem and certain microscopic characteristics. See also *Psilocybe cyanescens* and *Psilocybe baeocystis.*

Microscopic characters: Spores 9–12(13) x 5.5–6.5 μ. Basidia 4-spored. Pleurocystidia absent. Cheilocystidia present.

» *P. stuntzii*   GUZMÁN AND OTT

Cap: 1.5–4(5) cm broad. Cap obtusely conic at first, soon expanding to convex to broadly convex-umbonate to nearly flattened or plane with the margin uplifting in very mature fruiting bodies. Margin translucent-striate halfway to the disc when moist; decurved , then straightening, and finally elevated, undulating, and often eroded in extreme age. Dark chestnut brown, lighter towards the margin which is often olive-greenish; hygrophanous, fading to a more yellowish brown to pale yellow in drying. Some varieties tend to be more olive yellowish brown and are not very hygrophanous. Context relatively thin, watery brown or nearly concolorous with the cap. Surface viscid when moist from a separable gelatinous pellicle.

Gills: Attachment adnate to adnexed, close to subdistant, moderately broad, with three tiers of intermediate gills. Color pallid in young fruiting bodies, soon becoming more brownish and eventually very dark brown with spore maturity.

Stem: 3–6 cm long by 2–4 mm thick. Subequal, slightly enlarged at the apex and often curved and inflated at the base. (In some specimens, the stem will be extremely contorted in a 'pig's tail' fashion.) Dingy yellow to pale yellowish brown. Surface dry, covered with pallid appressed fibrils to the annulus, and smooth above. Context stuffed with a fibrous whitish pith. Partial veil thinly membranous, typically streaked bluish, leaving a fragile membranous annulus as the cap expands, which soon deteriorates into a fairly persistent annular zone darkened by spores. Stem often with rhizomorphs protruding about the base.

Growth habit and habitat: Growing in gregarious to subcespitose clusters on wood chips or in decayed conifer substratum, also in lawns and fields, in the fall to early winter, and in the spring. Reported from western Washington and British Columbia. Abundant throughout the Puget Sound area. It is likely *P. stuntzii* grows in Oregon as well.

Comments: Contains psilocybin and psilocin. By weight, *P. stuntzii* is one of the weaker of the bluing psilocybes. This species often grows in colonies of great numbers and was newly named in honor of Dr. Daniel Stuntz, who made the type collections. The field variety of this species is yet to be named at this writing. The *P. stuntzii* group encompasses a great variety of forms growing in varied habitats. See also *Galerina autumnalis* and *Naematoloma ericaeum.*

Microscopic characters: Spores (8)9–10.5(12.5) x 6–7(8) x 5.5–6.5 μ. Basidia 4-spored. Pleurocystidia absent. Cheilocystidia present, causing the gill edge to be heteromorphic.

» *P. subviscida*   (PECK) KAUFFMAN

Cap: .5–1.5(2) cm broad. Campanulate expanding with age to convex-umbonate or broadly convex while retaining an obtuse umbo. Margin translucent-striate when moist. Chestnut brown to reddish brown, fading in drying to pale grayish yellow and usually with the umbo remaining reddish brown. Surface viscid to subviscid when moist and soon drying.

Gills: Attachment adnate, subdistant, and broad. Whitish at first, soon becoming dark brownish.

Stem: 2–4 cm long by 1–2 mm thick. Equal to tapering downwards near the base. Surface covered at first with fine whitish fibrils. Partial veil thin to obscure, leaving an evanescent annular zone of fibrils usually darkened by spores if at all present.

Growth habit and habitat: Usually found growing in grassy areas, in well manured grounds, or in dung. Also reported to grow in mossy areas and in decayed conifer substratum. Typically found growing in the spring. Reported from Michigan and California. Thought to be widely distributed.

Comments: It is interesting for a species to inhabit such a wide spectrum of habitats. Edibility undocumented. See also *Psilocybe montana, Psilocybe merdaria,* and *Psilocybe angustispora.*

Microscopic characters: Spores 6–7 x 4–5 μ. Basidia 4-spored. Pleurocystidia not recorded. Cheilocystidia present.

» *P. thrausta*
(SCHULZER EX KALCHBREMER) ORTON

Cap: 3–7 cm broad. Obtusely conic at first, soon becoming convex to broadly convex, and finally nearly plane with or without an umbo. Viscid when moist from a gelatinous pellicle that is usually separable, soon drying. Orangish red to reddish brown or brick red. Margin initially ornamented with small scales, soon becoming smooth.

Gills: Attachment adnate to adnexed, sometimes uncinate, close to subdistant, moderately broad, with two to three tiers of intermediate gills. Pallid gray at first, soon becoming grayish brown and eventually dark purplish brown when fully mature.

Stem: 5–10(12) cm long by 3–7(8) mm thick. Nearly equal to swollen and often curved at the base. Hollow in age. Pallid towards the apex and more brownish near the base. Covered with floccose scales at first to the annulus and usually with orangish rhizomorphs protruding about the base. Partial veil membranous, fragile, leaving a superior membranous annulus often absent in age.

Growth habit and habitat: Scattered in the fall in decayed wood substratum or wood debris. Reported from the Pacific Northwest and Maryland. It is probably widely distributed across the continent.

Comments: Edibility uncertain. This species was once considered a variety of *S. squamosa* (now a *Psilocybe*) and is very similar to it in appearance, differing in the cap coloration. *Naematoloma aurantiaca*, another brick red colored mushroom, closely resembles this species as well.

Microscopic characters: Spores close to *P. squamosa* in size, but with an eccentric germ pore. Basidia 4-spored. Cheilocystidia present. Pleurocystidia absent.

» *P. umbonatescens* (PECK) SACCARDO

Cap: 1–4 cm broad. Conic-campanulate with a distinct umbo. Margin decorated with fragile whitish remnants of the partial veil. Yellowish to pale ochraceous brown toward the disc. Surface viscid when moist from a separable gelatinous pellicle. Flesh thin, pallid.

Gills: Attachment adnate to subdecurrent, close, broad. Color whitish at first, then grayish, and eventually purplish brown.

Stem: 5–10 cm long. Equal and slender. Pallid to yellowish, lighter than the cap. Surface initially covered with fine fibrils but soon smooth. Partial veil thinly membranous, floccose, leaving an obscure evanescent annular zone of fibrils, if at all.

Growth habit and habitat: Gregarious on dung in the fall in the Pacific Northwest.

Comments: Similar to *Stropharia semiglobata*. Further study needs to be made to clear up some ambiguities surrounding the *P. umbonatescens* group.

Microscopic characters: Spores 15–19 x 10 μ. Basidia 2-spored. Cheilocystidia and pleurocystidia present.

» *P. washingtonensis* SMITH

Cap: 1–2 cm broad. Obtusely conic to convex. Margin incurved at first, then straight. Deep 'walnut' brown and lighter towards the margin, fading to dull cinnamon or pale pecan in drying. Surface smooth though the margin may be ornamented with faint remnants of the veil, viscid when moist from a gelatinous pellicle, separable only in shreds when wet. Context thin, pliant, and nearly concolorous with the cap when moist.

Gills: Attachment adnate or subdecurrent, close to subdistant, with two or three tiers of intermediate gills. Color slightly darker than the cap at maturity.

Stem: 3–5 cm long by 1.5–2.5 mm thick. Equal, tubular, and pliant. At first same color as the cap but becoming blackish brown in age from the base upwards. Surface covered with grayish fibrils. Partial veil thinly cortinate.

Growth habit and habitat: Scattered to gregarious directly on decayed conifer wood in the fall. Reported from the Olympic Peninsula of Washington.

Comments: Edibility not documented. See also *N. dispersum*, *P. silvatica* and *P. pelliculosa*.

Microscopic characters: Spores 6–7.5(8) x 4–4.5 μ. Basidia 4-spored. Pleurocystidia present. Cheilocystidia present with two distinct types.

THE GENUS *STROPHARIA* (FRIES) QUÉLET

The genus *Stropharia* is closely related to both *Naematoloma* and *Psilocybe*. Species of *Stropharia* often possess membranous annuli on the stems and most have *naematolomoid chrysocystidia* cells on the gills. *Stropharia* species can be found in a wide range of terrestrial habitats but rarely grow in cespitose clusters or directly on wood. Some stropharias could be mistaken for species of *Agaricus*, if not for the fact that the gills of *Stropharia* are attached to the stem and have purplish-brown spore deposits, whereas species of *Agaricus* have gills which are free from the stem and have spore deposits that are more chocolate brown in color. *Pholiota* and *Agrocybe* are also similar in stature but have dull brown to earth brown spores. One species, *Stropharia rugosoannulata*, the wine-red *Stropharia*, is edible and choice. Many species of this genus are suspected and their edibility is uncertain. Species of the *Stropharia aeruginosa* complex may be hallucinogenic, and *Stropharia coronilla* and *Stropharia hornemannii* are suspected to be poisonous.

» *S. aeruginosa* (CURTIS EX FRIES) QUÉLET

Cap: 1–7 cm broad. Convex to convex-campanulate in age. Margin often decorated with whitish remains of the partial veil. Deep bluish to bright bluish green, often becoming more yellowish green with maturity and in drying. Surface viscid when moist from a separable gelatinous pellicle, sometimes adorned with scales, soon disappearing. Flesh whitish and soft, occasionally tinted bluish.

Gills: Attachment adnate, close, broad, with edges that may be minutely hairy and whitish. Color grayish at first, then becoming light purplish brown.

Stem: 3–8 cm long by 3–10 mm thick. Equal and having an overall stout appearance. Whitish above the annulus and greenish blue below. Surface sometimes scaly at first, soon smooth and usually viscid below the annulus. Partial veil soft and membranous, leaving a superior but fragile well-formed membranous annulus often not present in age.

Growth habit and habitat: Gregarious to cespitose in grassy areas, in bushy places, and in decayed conifer substratum. Widely dispersed throughout the continent.

Comments: The taste is reportedly disagreeable and this species has been thought to be poisonous. Several species are included in the complex surrounding *S. aeruginosa*. *S. cyanea* bruises bluish green and there is evidence this species is psilocybian. Caution is definitely recommended for all the members of this group. *Stropharia albocyanea*, a very rare species, has a more whitish stem, a lighter cap with slight bluish green tints, and is smaller; otherwise it is very similar to this species. The validity of the epithet *albocyanea* is questioned and more work needs to be done with this species. *Pholiota subcaerula* is commonly mistaken for *S. aeruginosa* and differs in the color of the spore deposit.

Microscopic characters: Spores 7–10 x 4–5 μ. Basidia 4-spored. Cheilocystidia present. Pleurocystidia present.

» *S. albocyanea* (DESMAZ) QUÉLET

Cap: Generally less than 4 cm broad at maturity. Cap obtusely conic to convex at first, soon expanding to broadly convex, and finally plane. Margin often appendiculate with whitish remnants of the partial veil. Pale whitish to pale yellowish with slight bluish tints in mature fruiting bodies, more bluish in very young specimens.

Gills: Attachment adnexed to sinuate, close to crowded, and moderately broad. Becoming pale purplish to purplish brown at maturity.

Stem: 2–6 cm long by 2–4 mm thick. Equal to curved at the base. Surface covered with slight fibrils below the annulus, smooth above, and dry. Whitish to pallid overall. Partial veil membranous, leaving a fairly persistent membranous annulus in the superior region of the stem, darkened with spores.

Growth habit and habitat: Growing during the fall in decayed wood substratum, in meadows, and according to M.C. Cooke, in dung. Collected in Washington, thought to be widely distributed, especially in the West.

Comments: Also known as *S. pseudocyanea* Desm., the authenticity of this species remains controversial. Some mycologists consider it a distinct species while other see *S. albocyanea* a form of *S. aeruginosa*. In any event, it is very rare. The edibility is not documented and caution is certainly recommended. See *S. aeruginosa*. *Pholiota subcaerula* resembles this group in a general sense.

Microscopic characters: I have not found any microscopic data for this species in the literature. I would expect it to ber similar to *S. aeruginosa*.

» *S. albonitens* (FRIES) QUÉLET

Cap: 1–3 cm broad. Broadly campanulate expanding to nearly plane, often with an umbo. Whitish to buff, occasionally tinged yellowish towards the center. Surface smooth, viscid when moist from a gelatinous pellicle. Flesh thin and whitish.

Gills: Attachment adnate to uncinate, subdistant, moderately broad, edges minutely fringed and whitish. Color gray to purplish gray.

Stem: 3–7 cm long by 2–3 mm thick. Whitish at first and then yellowish with age. Surface finely 'wooly' to pruinose. Flesh stuffed with a whitish pith, becoming hollow with age. Partial veil whitish and membranous, usually leaving an evanescent annular zone of fibrils soon colored by spores.

Growth habit and habitat: Scattered on the ground in open grassy woods in the fall. This species has been collected in Michigan and in California. It is probably widely distributed.

Comments: Edibility is suspected. Distinguished from similar species by the grayish color of the gills and the yellowish color of the stem in age. See also *S. bilamellata*.

Microscopic characters: Spores 7–9 x 4–5 μ. Basidia 4-spored. Cheilocystidia and pleurocystidia not recorded.

» *S. ambigua* (PECK) ZELLER

Cap: 2–10 cm broad. Obtuse to convex when young with an inrolled margin, becoming broadly convex to nearly plane with age. Margin decorated with floccose white scales (appendiculate from remnants of the partial veil), soon becoming smooth. Dull yellowish brown to pale or bright yellow in maturity.

Surface viscid when moist from a separable gelatinous pellicle. Flesh thick and white.

Gills: Attachment mostly adnate, sometimes adnexed or uncinate, close, moderately broad , and with even edges. Color whitish at first, then grayish, and eventually dark purplebrown.

Stem: 8–15 cm long by 8–15 mm thick. Equal to slightly enlarged at the base. Surface whitish, striated at the apical area, with the lower regions having the remains of the veil attached or with distinct whitish scales to the annular region. Soon smooth overall. In age dull grayish to yellowish. Flesh stuffed with a whitish pith. Partial veil fragile, white, and membranous, sometimes leaving a very evanescent membranous annulus, but soon deteriorating to an obscure annular zone, if at all present. Numerous white rhizomorphs present about the base of the stem.

Growth habit and habitat: Solitary to gregarious in conifer woods on humus or duff, also found under alder in river valleys. Mostly occurring in the fall to early winter and to a lesser degree in the spring. Reported throughout western North America, particularly abundant in the Pacific Northwest and to a lesser degree in California.

Comments: Thought to be edible, but one should observe the usual precautions for eating a mushroom for the first time. Sterile forms of this species develop bright yellow gills. Purportedly tastes like old leaves. See also *S. hornemannii* and *Psilocybe squamosa*.

Microscopic characters: Spores 11–14 x 6–7.5 μ. Basidia 4-spored. Cheilocystidia present. Pleurocystidia present, but not conspicuous.

» *S. bilamellata* PECK

Cap: 2.5–5 cm broad. Convex at first and nearly plane in age. Whitish or yellowish overall. Surface smooth, even. Flesh pure white.

Gills: Attachment adnate, close, thin. Color purplish brown at maturity.

Stem: 2.5 cm long by 6–8 mm thick. Whitish overall. Context solid at first, and may become hollow in age, especially in large carpophores. Partial veil membranous, leaving a well-developed persistent membranous annulus that has pronounced gill-like grooves on its upperside.

Growth habit and habitat: Scattered in grass, shrubs, or in cultivated fields. Reported from Washington, California, New York, North Carolina, and Alabama.

Comments: This species resembles *S. coronilla* and is distinguished from it by the gilled annulus. Edibility is not documented.

Microscopic characters: Spores 10 x 5–6 μ. Basidia 4-spored. Cheilocystidia present. Pleurocystidia absent.

» *S. coronilla*
(BULLIARD EX FRIES) QUÉLET

Cap: 1–4(6) cm broad. Hemispheric to convex, becoming nearly plane. Yellowish brown to straw yellow. Surface smooth, viscid when very moist, otherwise only slightly viscid to lubricous when moist. Flesh thick and white.

Gills: Attachment adnate, can be sinuate in age, close and moderately broad. Color whitish at first, soon becoming strongly violet or purplish brown.

Stem: 2–4 cm long by 3–5 mm thick. Equal and short in stature overall. Mostly whitish. Surface minutely 'wooly' above annulus and fibrillose below, eventually becoming smooth. Partial veil membranous, leaving a persistent white annulus in the center of the stem and slightly striated on the upperside. Whitish rhizomorphs often present at base.

Growth habit and habitat: Scattered to numerous in grassy areas such as lawns and fields in the late summer and fall throughout the Pacific Northwest and in California. It is probably widely distributed across the continent.

Comments: Weather conditions greatly affect the viscidity of the cap of this species. The taste is mild, but edibility is suspect and therefore not recommended. *Stropharia coronilla* is very close to *Stropharia melanosperma*, which has a thicker stem at maturity and larger spores. See also *S. bilamellata*.

Microscopic characters: Spores 7–9.5 x 4–5 μ. Basidia 4-spored. Cheilocystidia and pleurocystidia present.

» *S. hardii* ATKINS

Cap: 5–9 cm broad at maturity. Convex at first, soon expanding to broadly convex and eventually plane. Margin even, sometimes slightly undulated and irregular when fully mature. Pale to bright ochraceous in overall color, often with darkened regions or 'spots'. Viscid when moist, soon drying.

Gills: Attachment adnexed, crowded, and moderately broad. Dark brown to purplish brown in age.

Stem: Approximately 4–8 cm long by 5–15 mm thick. Equal to tapering into a short pseudorhiza at the base, soon becoming hollow. Pallid to yellowish overall. Partial veil membranous, leaving a persistent membranous annulus in the superior region of the stem. Surface viscid to glutinous below the annulus and covered with fragile floccose scales.

Growth habit and habitat: Growing scattered, mostly in grassy areas and in decayed wood substratum of the southeastern United States in the spring and fall.

Comments: Edibility unknown. The viscid or glutinous scaly stem is an important feature taxonomically. See *S. hornemannii.*

Microscopic characters: Spores 5–9 x 3–5 μ. Basidia 4-spored. Pleurocystidia present. Cheilocystidia present, similar to pleurocystidia but smaller.

» *S. hornemannii*
(FRIES) LUNDELL ET NANNFELDT

Cap: 6–12 cm broad. Obtuse to convex, becoming broadly convex to plane at maturity. Margin incurved at first in young carpophores and may elevate in age; occasionally translucent-striate with white cottony scales along the edge. Color dull brown to light purplish gray to smoky reddish brown and often becoming a more yellowish brown with age. Surface viscid to glutinous when wet from a thick gelatinous hyaline or yellowish separable pellicle, soon becoming smooth and free of veil remnants.

Gills: Attachment adnate to uncinate, close to subdistant, broad, with three tiers of intermediate gills, and even edges. Color pallid or grayish at first, then dull purple-brown with spore maturity.

Stem: 5–15 cm long by 8–25 mm thick. Nearly equal, thicker at the apex, and eventually becoming hollow. Surface covered with conspicuous cottony white scales to the annulus, smooth and silky above. Well formed membranous annulus present, upturned at first, downturned and often torn in age. White rhizomorphs protruding about the base of the stem.

Growth habit and habitat: Single to gregarious or rarely in clusters of two or three in well decayed conifer substratum, logs, and stumps in the fall throughout the Pacific Northwest and California.

Comments: The taste is disagreeable and this species is not recommended. It may be poisonous. See also *S. hardii*. In the past, there has been some confusion with species closely allied to *S. hornemannii*, particularly *S. depilata* (Persoon) Saccardo, which is now considered synonymous.

Microscopic characters: Spores 10.5–13 x 5.5–7 μ. Basidia 4-spored. Pleurocystidia (some chrysocystidia) present. Cheilocystidia present.

» *S. kauffmanii* SMITH

Cap: 6–15 cm broad. Broadly convex to plane at maturity. Margin incurved at first but soon straightening. Sometimes appendiculate with remnants of the partial veil. Yellowish with brownish recurved scales. Surface densely fibrillose scaly and dry. Flesh thick, white, and soft but not fragile.

Gills: Depressed adnate, or at times uncinate, crowded, narrow, and often with eroded edges. Color pallid but soon becoming dark brownish.

Stem: 6–10 cm long by 1.5–3 mm thick. More or less equal, often compressed, hollow, and firm. Surface whitish or 'cream color' towards the base, with upright pointed to fibrillose scales. Superior nonpersistent membranous annulus present and with numerous white rhizomorphs protruding about the base of the stem.

Growth habit and habitat: Singly to gregarious under piles of brush of alder, maple, and cottonwood in the spring and fall. Known from Washington.

Comments: This species is distinguished by its dry, scaly cap. In appearance, it has affinities to some pholiotas. See also *S. magnivelaris* and *Psilocybe squamosa*.

Microscopic characters: Spores 6–7 x 4–4.5 μ. Basidia 4-spored. Cheilocystidia present. Pleurocystidia absent.

» *S. magnivelaris* PECK

Cap: 3–5.5 cm broad. Obtusely umbonate to convex at first, then broadly convex to plane in age. Margin appendiculate from remnants of the partial veil and may be elevated in older carpophores. Surface occasionally adorned with fibrillose scales near the margin, soon smooth, and viscid when moist from a thin gelatinous pellicle. Color 'cream buff' (pale grayish-yellow), not particularly hygrophanous. Flesh moderately thick (3–4 mm), firm, and whitish.

Gills: Attachment adnate, broad, close, and with three tiers of intermediate gills. Color pale yellow to brownish with spore maturity.

Stem: 6–9 cm long by 4–7 mm thick. Equal to mostly enlarged above. Color whitish or may be sordid brown in age. Surface with fibrillose patches below annulus, smooth above. Partial veil thickly membranous, leaving a well-formed, flaring membranous annulus that is fairly persistent.

Growth habit and habitat: Scattered to gregarious in the spring on sandy soil of river flats under alder. Reported from the Olympic Peninsula of Washington State.

Comments: Edibility is not documented. It seems this species should belong to the genus *Psilocybe* rather than *Stropharia* for the absence of chrysocystidia on its gills. *S. magnivelaris* is also known as *S. percevalii* (Berk. and Br.) Sacc. See also *S. ambigua*, *S. kauffmanii*, and *Psilocybe squamosa*.

Microscopic characters: Spores 13–14 (15) x 6–8 μ. Basidia 4-spored. Cheilocystidia present. Pleurocystidia absent.

» *S. melanosperma* (BULLIARD) QUÉLET

Cap: 3.5–4.5 cm broad at maturity. Convex, expanding to broadly convex and eventually plane. Surface smooth overall, slightly viscid when moist and soon drying, often cracking in the process. Pallid to whitish, tending to straw yellow at the disc area.

Gills: Attachment adnate to adnexed, crowded, and broad. Pallid to grayish at first, becoming dark purplish gray-black when fully mature.

Stem: 4–6 (7) cm long by 6–7 mm thick. Equal, straight, and hollow. Surface smooth. Pallid to whitish overall. Partial veil membranous, leaving a fairly persistent membranous annulus soon colored by spores.

Growth habit and habitat: Growing in dung or in well manured grounds in the spring and fall. Essentially an eastern species, reported from New England, New York, extending as far south as Texas. It is probably widely distributed throughout the East. There are no known reports of this species occurring in the West.

Comments: Edibility is not documented. As with any species whose edibility is unknown, caution is recommended. Close to *S. bilamellata, S. coronilla,* and *S. albonitens* in general appearance.

Microscopic characters: Spores 12 x 7–8 μ. Cheilocystidia and pleurocystidia present.

» *S. rugoso-annulata*
FARLOW EX MURRILL

Cap: 4.5–13 cm broad. Convex to obtusely campanulate, expanding to convex, finally plane. Margin tending to remain incurved. Surface fibrillose and dry. Wine red to reddish brown at first, soon becoming grayish red-brown, often fading to pallid yellowish-brown with age. Flesh thick, soft, and whitish.

Gills: Attachment adnate or adnexed, seceding eventually to lend the appearance of being free, thin, crowded, and with several tiers of intermediate gills. Edges even. Color whitish at first, soon becoming gray and then dark purplish gray with whitish edges at maturity.

Stem: 7.5–10.5 cm long by 10–25 mm thick. Nearly equal above and with a thickened to bulbous base that has long rhizomorphs attached to it. Surface smooth to appressed fibrillose to scaly below annulus and sometimes striate above. Whitish, staining yellowish in age. Partial veil leaving a thick persistent membranous annulus, radially split with gill-like grooves on the upperside in the superior region of the stem.

Growth habit and habitat: Scattered to gregarious on cultivated ground in the spring, summer, and fall. Reported from Massachusetts and Washington and probably to be found elsewhere in the Northeastern United States and in the Pacific Northwest.

Comments: Edible and choice. Known as the Wine Red *Stropharia,* it is one of the largest species in this genus. Because of the seceding gills, this species could be mistaken for an *Agaricus* if the collector did not take into account the dark purplish gray color of the gills at maturity, the spore deposit, and the original gill attachment. It has been successfully cultivated on composted straw.

Microscopic characters: Spores 13.5–15 x 8–9 μ. Basidia 4-spored. Cheilocystidia present. Pleurocystidia (as chrysocystidia) present.

» *S. semiglobata* (FRIES) QUÉLET

Cap: 1–4 cm broad. Obtuse to hemispheric to convex and finally broadly convex in age. Occasionally with an umbo. Light yellow to deep straw yellow. Surface smooth, extremely viscid to glutinous when moist from a separable gelatinous pellicle. Flesh firm, watery buff, thickest at the disc and thinning towards the margins.

Gills: Attachment adnate, broad, close to subdistant, with one to two tiers of intermediate gills. Edges whitish and fringed. Color grayish when young, becoming dark purple-grayish brown.

Stem: 3–12 cm long by 2–5 mm thick. Equal to slightly enlarged downwards to the base. Surface below annular zone typically whitish to nearly concolorous with the cap. Extremely viscid to glutinous in the lower two-thirds from a glutinous universal veil. Partial veil also glutinous, soon breaking, and leaving an evanescent annular zone usually darkened with spores. Flesh stuffed with a yellowish pith at first and then becoming hollow with aging.

Growth habit and habitat: Single to gregarious on cow or horse dung in the spring, summer, and fall. Widely distributed throughout the North American continent.

Comments: Inedible. Frequently found with *Psilocybe coprophila. S. semiglobata* is one of the most commonly encountered of dung-inhabiting fungi along with *Panaelous sphinctrinus.* See also *S. siccipes, S. stercoraria, Psilocybe umbonatescens,* and *Psilocybe semilanceata.*

Microscopic characters: Spores 15–18 x 9–10 μ. Basidia 4-spored. Cheilocystidia present. Pleurocystidia (chrysocystidia) present.

» *S. semigloboides* MURRILL

Cap: 2–4.5 cm broad. Obtusely conic, becoming convex to plane with age. margin faintly striate. 'Honey' yellow to deep yellowish. Surface glutinous from a thick separable gelatinous pellicle and smooth. Flesh moderately thick (3–4 mm) and thinning towards the margin.

Gills: Attachment adnate, soon seceding,

moderately broad, close, and with even edges. At first whitish, then pallid brownish.

Stem: 8–11 cm long by 4–5 mm thick. More or less equal above, tubular, and tapering downwards into a long pseudorhiza (a root-like prolongation). Surface covered by a glutinous sheath to the evanescent annular zone, and pruinose above. Yellowish towards the apex and whitish to pallid towards the base. Partial veil gelatinous.

Growth habit and habitat: Singly to scattered on humus under spruce. Reported from Oregon and probably occurring elsewhere in the Pacific Northwest. Found during the fall.

Comments: Edibility not documented.

Microscopic characters: Spores 8–10 x 4–5 μ. Basidia 4-spored. Cheilocystidia present. Pleurocystidia present but hard to find.

» *S. siccipes* KARSTEN

Cap: 2–3 cm broad. Hemispheric at first, expanding to nearly plane. Margin even and translucent striate. Clay-white to yellowish in drying. Surface viscid when moist. Flesh relatively thick at the disc and thinner towards the margin.

Gills: Attachment adnate to subdecurrent. Color clay colored to dark brownish gray in age.

Stem: 4–7 cm long by 2 mm thick. More or less equal, flexuous, and often tapering into a pseudorhiza. Whitish to pale whitish overall. Surface dry; flocculose above annulus, smooth below. Flesh stuffed with a pith at first and soon becoming hollow with maturity. Partial veil thin to rudimentary, leaving a fibrillose annular zone soon darkened by spores.

Growth habit and habitat: Scattered on dung or on well-manured ground in the spring. Widely distributed across the North American continent.

Comments: Similar to *S. semiglobata* and *S. stercoraria* but the stem is dry, not glutinous,

and tapers into a pseudorhiza in many collections. See also *S. albonitens.*

Microscopic characters: Spores 12–15 x 7–9 μ. Basidia 4-spored. Cheilocystidia and pleurocystidia present.

» *S. stercoraria* (HUDSON) MURRILL

Cap: 2–5 cm broad. Obtusely conic at first, then hemispheric, soon expanding to broadly convex to plane. Margin incurved at first, even, straightening as the cap expands, and may be slightly undulated in very mature carpophores (fruiting bodies). Yellowish at first, becoming lighter near the margin with whitish hues. Surface smooth, viscid when moist.

Gills: Attachment adnate to uncinate, broad, and close to crowded. Whitish at first, then brownish to dark purplish brown with a slight olivaceous cast in age with the edges remaining whitish fringed.

Stem: 6 cm or longer in mature carpophores. Equal to slightly enlarged at the base. Flesh stuffed with a pith at first and becoming hollow with age. Surface dry or subviscid when moist (not glutinous), and finely 'wooly' below annular zone. Partial veil yellowish and thinly membranous though very fragile, soon disappearing, leaving a slight evanescent annular zone.

Growth habit and habitat: Growing in the dung of domesticated animals or on well-manured grounds. Widely distributed throughout the North American continent.

Comments: Very close in appearance to *S. semiglobata* but is not as persistently hemispheric as this species—the cap soon expands to nearly plane, the partial veil is not glutinous, and the spores are slightly olivaceous in 2½% KOH when viewed through a microscope. Some authors consider *S. semiglobata* and *S. stercoraria* to be synonymous.

Microscopic characters: Spores 15–21 x 8–12 μ. Basidia 4-spored. Cheilocystidia and pleurocystidia present.

The Coprinaceae

THE GENUS *PANAEOLUS* (FRIES) QUÉLET

The genera *Panaeolus, Psathyrella,* and *Coprinus* belong to the family Coprinaceae. Most psilocybian species of this family are in *Panaeolus.* Species of

Panaeolus are known by the mottled or 'spotted' appearance of their gills, just prior to being fully mature. This phenomenon is caused by uneven ripening of spore producing cells (called *basidia*) on the gill surfaces (see Appendix 1). Many of the species in this genus grow in dung, while only a few North American panaeoli are non-coprophilic, preferring grassy or lignicolous habitats. *Psathyrella* is quite similar in appearance to *Panaeolus*, but usually species of this genus grow in decayed wood substrata and in soil. Also the caps of psathyrellas tend to be more striate than those of panaeoli. Chemically, *Panaeolus* spores do not fade or discolor in concentrated sulphuric acid while *Psathyrella* spores do. The coprini are very distinct in the plicate (folded) nature of their caps and the fact that most species *deliquesce* at spore maturity (a process of autodigestion whereby the cap is reduced to a black liquid or becomes paper thin).

Following Dr. Rolf Singer's interpretation of this family there are at least three other genera stemming from the traditional notion of the genus *Panaeolus*. Under the subfamily Panaeoloideae, he lists *Panaeolina* (species with roughened spores including *P. foenisecii* and presumably *P. castaneifolius*), *Copelandia* (generally tropical or semi-tropical species readily bruising bluish green, including *P. cyanescens* and *tropicalis*), *Anellaria* (large fleshy whitish species, often with viscid caps, including *P. semiovatus* and *P. phalaenarum*); the remaining species not fitting into any of these categories are considered the true *Panaeolus*. Dr. Gastón Guzmán's treatment of the genus (in 1972) seems the most sensible. He calls each of the above named groups 'subgenera' within *Panaeolus*. For taxonomic clarity I consider these genera or subgenera to be accurately represented under the epithet of one genus, *Panaeolus*. Several species are consistent or latent producers of psilocybin and/or psilocin, though none are poisonous.

» *P. acuminatus* (SCHAEFFER) QUÉLET

Cap: 1.5–2.5 (4.0) cm broad. Conic to conic-campanulate, becoming more campanulate to convex and in extreme age expanding to plane. Margin appendiculate with fine fibrils if at all, distinctly translucent-striate when moist, incurved when young and soon straightening. Cap chestnut or deep reddish brown when moist, hygrophanous, becoming more tawny in fading from the apex and remaining darker along the margin. Surface smooth, viscid to lubricous when wet, soon drying.

Gills: Attachment adnate to adnexed, close to crowded, broad, and even. Several tiers of intermediate gills present. Very dark purplish gray-black at maturity and mottled.

Stem: 4.5–10.5 (15.0) cm long by 2.5–6.5 mm thick. Equal to slightly enlarged at the base or at the apex, tubular, and more or less brittle (cartilaginous). Very dark reddish brown or nearly concolorous with the cap.

Surface pruinose and often with small water droplets adhering near to the apex of the stem.

Growth habit and habitat: Growing scattered to gregariously in grassy areas and in well manured grounds or on dung in the spring and fall throughout North America. I often find this species in the field-forest interface.

Comments: Not believed to be hallucinogenic. *P. rickenii* is similar but has a parabolic cap in younger stages of development. See also *P. foenisecii* and *P. castaneifolius*.

Microscopic characters: Spores 12–16 x 7.5–11.0 μ. Basidia 4-spored, rarely 2-spored. Cheilocystidia present. Pleurocystidia absent.

» *P. campanulatus* (FRIES) QUÉLET

Cap: (1) 2–5 (6) cm broad. Obtusely conic becoming campanulate with age and having a margin decorated with whitish tooth-like remnants of the partial veil. Occasionally with an obtuse umbo. Brownish to reddish brown, often with some grayish hues, and finally grayish cinnamon buff, while often remaining more tawny at the disc. Not particularly hygrophanous (fading in drying). Surface relatively smooth in young fruiting bodies and may be finely wrinkled in very mature specimens, moist to lubricous when wet but soon dry. Flesh thickest under the cap and thinning towards the margins; nearly concolorous with the cap.

Gills: Attachment adnexed and soon seceding from the stem, close to subdistant, moderately broad, with 1–2 tiers of intermediate gills. Color grayish at first, becoming mottled dark grayish black from the uneven ripening of the spores.

Stem: 6–14 cm long by 1.5–3.5(5) mm thick. Equal, tubular, fibrous, and slightly striate towards the apex. Overall color brownish under a grayish pruinose surface.

Growth habit and habitat: Growing scattered to gregariously on dung in the fall or spring throughout North America.

Comments: Along with *P. sphinctrinus,* this mushroom is undoubtedly one of the most commonly found of dung-inhabiting *Panaeolus.* It is not known to be active in North America. *Panaeolus campanulatus* and *Panaeolus sphinctrinus* are two very closely related species comprising a taxonimically difficult complex of mushrooms.

Microscopic characters: Spores 13–18 x 7.5–12 μ. Basidia 4-spored. Cheilocystidia present, causing the gill edge to be heteromorphic. Pleurocystidia not observed.

» *P. castaneifolius* (MURRILL) OLA'H

Cap: 1.0–3.0(4) cm broad. Distinctly campanulate at first, soon subhemispheric, then convex and becoming broadly convex in age. Margin incurved at first, soon straightening, not appendiculate, and slightly striated. Dark smoky gray when moist, hygrophanous, soon drying to a more straw-yellow or pale ochraceous, and remaining more reddish brown at the apex and more smoky brownish along the margin. Surface sometimes finely wrinkled.

Gills: Attachment adnate to adnexed, close, and thin. Pallid at first, becoming dark purplish gray-black at spore maturity.

Stem: 4–6(7.5) cm long by 3–4(6) mm thick. Equal to more narrow towards the base. Hollow or tubular; and brittle. Grayish

to ochraceous or tan at the base. Surface slightly striated, pruinose.

Growth habit and habitat: Growing scattered to gregariously in grassy areas across the North American continent.

Comments: Latently psilocybian. Some collections of this species contain psilocybin. Distinguished from *Panaeolus foenisecii* by the color of the mature gills and spore deposit, which are very dark purplish gray-black.

Microscopic characters: Spores finely roughened, 12–15 x 7–9.5 μ. Basidia 4-spored. Cheilocystidia present. Pleurocystidia few, or absent, not projecting beyond basidia.

» *P. cyanescens* BERKELEY AND BROOME

Cap: 1.5–3.5(4) cm broad. Hemispheric to campanulate to convex at maturity. Margin initially translucent-striate when wet, incurved only in young fruiting bodies. Becoming undulated and often split or irregular when cold. Light brown at first, becoming pallid gray or nearly white overall. Cap cracking horizontally in age and in drying. Flesh readily bruising bluish green.

Gills: Attachment adnexed, close, thin, with two or three tiers of intermediate gills. Mottled grayish black at maturity.

Stem: (6.5)8.5–11.5 cm long by 1.5–3.0 mm thick. Equal to bulbous at the base, tubular. Often grayish towards the apex, pale yellowish overall, then flesh colored to light brown towards the base; readily turning bluish when bruised. Partial veil absent.

Growth habit and habitat: Growing in dung in pastures and fields. Reported from Mexico and Florida, and is to be expected in semi-tropical environs of the Southeast; also suspected from Hawaii.

Comments: Psilocybin and/or psilocin containing. See also *P. tropicalis.*

Microscopic characters: Spores 12–14 x 8.5–11 μ. They appear to be granulated. Pleurocystidia present, 30–60(80) x 12–17(25) μ. Cheilocystidia present, gill edge heteromorphic, 11–15 x 3–5(6) μ.

» *P. fimicola* FRIES

Cap: 1–2(3) cm broad. Convex to campanulate, expanding to plane only during prolonged wet periods and in extreme age. Dingy gray to light grayish black, often with slight reddish hues, becoming paler in drying leaving a brown encircling zone along the margin. Margin striate when moist, not appendiculate. Surface smooth, and soon dry. Flesh moderately thick.

Gills: Attachment adnate to adnexed, broad, grayish, and mottled. Two to three tiers of intermediate gills present.

Stem: 6–10 cm long by 2 mm thick. Equal, hollow, soft, and fragile. Dingy pale to whitish, especially towards the apex. Surface pruinose (powdered) and striate.

Growth habit and habitat: Growing scattered in soil or dung from the late spring to summer and in the fall. Widely distributed across North America.

Comments: Latently psilocybian. This rare species is fairly distinctive in appearance. The lack of veil remnants adhering to the margin, and the grayish to light grayish black coloration of the cap which often has slight reddish hues at the disc, separates this species from other members of the genus. See also *P. subbalteatus* and *P. castaneifolius.*

Microscopic characters: Spores 11–14 x 7–9.5 μ. Basidia 4-spored. Cheilocystidia present. Pleurocystidia few.

» *P. foenisecii* (FRIES) KUHNER

Cap: 1–3 cm broad. Campanulate to convex with an incurved and occasionally translucent margin, especially in young fruiting bodies; expanding to broadly convex or nearly plane with age. Smoky brown to dull chestnut brown, hygrophanous, fading to sordid tan or light grayish brown, and often having a dark ring-like band along the margin. Surface smooth, and often cracking in drying. Flesh thin, watery brown when moist, pallid when dry.

Gills: Attachment adnate, and soon seceding, close, moderately broad, and slightly enlarged in the center. Color pallid in young fruiting bodies, darkening to a dull brownish or deep brown and becoming slightly mottled from the uneven ripening of the spores.

Stem: 4–8 cm long by 2–3.5 mm thick. Equal, brittle, pruinose, slightly striate and twisted towards the apex. Pallid to whitish overall, darkening brownish from the base upwards with age and after being handled. Veil obscure or absent.

Growth habit and habitat: Scattered to gregariously in grassy areas, never on dung.

Found most abundantly in the spring and to a lesser extent in the fall. Widely distributed.

Comments: This species is latently psilocybian. Apparently it is active in the eastern United States, but there are conflicting reports of its being active in the western United States. Macroscopically, some distinguishing features include its exclusive habitat in grass, the whitish striated stem, the occasional occurence of a darker marginal belt, and most of all the dark dull brownish gills. Microscopically, this is one of two species of *Panaeolus* found in western North America having rough spores. See also *Panaeolus castaneifolius.* Dr. Alexander Smith considered the two above named species to belong to *Psathyrella* in his monograph on this genus in 1972.

Microscopic characters: Spores rough, 12–17 x 7–9 μ. Cheilocystidia present, causing the gill edge to be heteromorphic. Pleurocystidia present in the form of chrysocystidia, but very difficult to find; not projecting beyond the basidia.

» *P. fontinalis* SMITH

Cap: 1–2.5 cm broad. Obtusely conic at first, expanding to convex with age. Deep olive yellowish brown to olive brown at first, lighter along the margin, and fading in drying to a light olive gray. Surface sometimes finely powdered, soon smooth, and dry or only moist when wet. Flesh thin and pallid.

Gills: Attachment adnexed, close, and relatively broad, usually with two tiers of intermediate gills inserted. Olive yellowish brown at first, soon darkening with age, becoming brown, then black and mottled from the uneven ripening of spores with the edges remaining whitish.

Stem: 5–10 cm long by 1–2 mm thick. Equal overall. Finely powdered at first, especially towards the apex, soon becoming smooth. Partial veil absent or rudimentary. Yellowish cinnamon brown to olive brown, more of a pallid color towards the apex.

Growth habit and habitat: Scattered on humus in a cedar swamp. Known only from Michigan.

Comments: Not hallucinogenic. The habitat and the olive hues of the maturing gills are considered taxonomically significant.

Microscopic characters: Spores 7–9 x 4–5 x 5–6.5 μ. Basidia 4-spored. Pleurocystidia scattered or absent. Cheilocystidia present, 26–34 x 6–9 μ.

» *P. fraxinophilus* SMITH

Cap: 5–15 mm broad. Conic at first, expanding to convex with age. Margin incurved at first and slightly translucent-striate when moist. Dark brownish gray to nearly black at the disc and more tawny towards the margin, hygrophanous, fading to sordid yellowish brown in drying. Flesh dark and thin.

Gills: Attachment adnexed to adnate, close, and moderately broad. Dull grayish brown becoming nearly black and mottled from the uneven ripening of spores.

Stem: 2–8 cm long by 1.5–2 mm thick. Equal overall, becoming hollow, and fragile. Partial veil absent to rudimentary. Dark grayish red-brown. Surface densely pruinose, often with beads of water attached in the upper regions.

Growth habit and habitats: Growing lignicolously on logs and stumps of fallen ash trees in the late summer and fall. Known from New York state and suspected to be more widely distributed throughout the Northeast.

Comments: Not hallucinogenic. This species is very distinct and unlikely to be confused with other mushrooms of the genus. Expect to find this mushroom along with *Coprinus disseminatus.*

Microscopic characters: Spores 9–11 x 5–6 x 6.5–7.5 μ. Basidia mostly 4-spored, some 2-spored. Pleurocystidia absent. Cheilocystidia present, 28–42 x 4–5 μ.

» *P. papilionaceus*
(BULLIARD EX FRIES) QUÉLET

Cap: 2–4 cm broad. Hemispheric, eventually expanding to broadly convex. Margin appendiculate at first from remnants of the partial veil, soon disappearing. Color pallid to smoky grayish or pallid brownish. Surface initially smooth, soon becoming cracked horizontally, giving the appearance of being scaly. Flesh moderately thick and whitish.

Gills: Attachment adnate, close, broad, and slightly swollen in the middle. Color mottled grayish black.

Stem: 4–8 cm long by 2–5 mm thick. Brittle, hollow. Whitish overall and more brownish towards the base. Surface powdered and striate at the apex.

Growth habit and habitat: Scattered to gregarious on dung in the fall and spring. Widely distributed.

Comments: Several reports say this species is hallucinogenic, while others do not. This species is *not* the same as *Copelandia papilonacea* (Bull. ex Fr.) Bres., or *P. cyanescens.* There is considerable taxonomic confusion surrounding *P. papilionaceus.* Some mycologists suspect it to be conspecific with *P. campanulatus.* Widely distributed across the continent.

Microscopic characters: Spores 15–18 x 9–11 μ. Basidia 4-spored. Cheilocystidia present. Pleurocystidia absent.

» *P. phalaenarum* (FRIES) QUÉLET

Cap: 4–10 cm broad. Hemispheric to broadly convex. Whitish at first and may become more yellowish towards the disc with age. Surface moist, smooth to rimose-scaly. Flesh relatively thick and whitish.

Gills: Attachment adnexed to adnate, close, broad, and slightly swollen in the center. Color whitish to grayish at first, soon darkening to mottled blackish.

Stem: 8–20 cm long by 5–15 mm thick. Equal to slightly enlarged and curved at the base, *solid,* and somewhat twisted. Whitish overall. Surface smooth to striate towards the apex. Context whitish.

Growth habit and habitat: Gregarious to subcespitose in the spring in the Pacific Northwest, British Columbia, and Alaska. It is probably widely distributed.

Comments: Edible. *P. phalaenarum* is synonymous with *P. solidipes* (Peck) Sacc., and closely allied to, if not synonomous with, *P. antillarum* (Fr.) Dennis. Similar to *P. semiovatus* in its relatively large stature. See also *P. sp.* and *P. papilionaceus.*

Microscopic characters: Spores 18–22 x 11–12.5 μ. Basidia 4-spored. Cheilocystidia present. Pleurocystidia present, of the chrysocystidia type.

» *P. retirugis* (FRIES) QUÉLET

Cap: 1–3 cm broad. Campanulate to hemispheric and often umbonate, at first with an appendiculate margin. Light to dark brownish with pinkish hues of a 'flesh tan' color. Surface often markedly wrinkled with dark interconnecting veins radiating outwards from the center of the cap. Flesh relatively thin.

Gills: Attachment adnate but soon seceding from the stem, close, broad, and slightly swollen in the center. Color blackish mottled from the uneven ripening of the spores with the edges remaining whitish at maturity.

Stem: 5–16 cm long by 2–6 mm thick. Equal, occasionally flexuous, and hollow. Tan to reddish purple and darker at the base.

Growth habit and habitat: Growing scattered to gregariously in dung or in hay in the fall or spring. Reported from throughout Western North America and thought to be widely distributed elsewhere.

Comments: The hallucinogenic properties of this species are not well understood. Some strains may be hallucinogenic. This species is distinguished by the wrinkled nature of the cap and its color tones. However, the wrinkled cap may not always be evident, especially in young specimens, and it could be confused with other appendiculate panaeoli. *P. campanulatus* and *P. sphinctrinus* are generally similar. The cap cuticle of *P. retirugis* is one cell thick while the cuticle of these previous two species is several cells thick.

Microscopic characters: Spores 11–16.5 x 8–10.5 μ. Basidia 4- and some 2-spored. Cheilocystidia present. Pleurocystidia absent.

» *P. rickenii* HORA

Cap: 8–20 mm broad. Parabolic at first, becoming obtusely conic to campanulate in age. Margin translucent-striate when moist. Surface smooth overall, often cracking in drying. Dark reddish brown to grayish red-brown, and hygrophanous; typically with a distinct, dark marginal zone or band when partly dry.

Gills: Attachment adnexed or ascending, crowded, and thin to moderately broad with one to three tiers of intermediate gills. Grayish at first, soon becoming dark purplish gray-black in age, and mottled from the uneven ripening of the spores. Margins pallid or whitish.

Stem: 4.5–7.0 cm long by 1–2 mm thick. Straight, equal to slightly enlarged and curved at the base. Surface covered with a fine whitish sheath of fibrils, more pruinose towards the apex, often with beads of water attached in moist conditions. Underlying tissue nearly

concolorous with the cap, or a bit lighter. Stuffed with a fibrous pith, becoming hollow in age.

Growth habit and habitat: Growing scattered to gregariously in grassy areas and in well manured grounds in the fall and to a lesser degree in the spring. Widely distributed across the continent.

Comments: Apparently not hallucinogenic. Closely allied to *P. acuminatus,* which ·has a conic cap when young and not parabolic as in this species. *P. acuminatus* and *P. rickenii* are naturally grouped together. There are probably unrecognized species clustered around these two.

Microscopic characters: Spores (8) 10–14 (15) x (7.5) 8.5–10 (11) μ. Basidia 4-spored. Cheilocystidia present. Pleurocystidia absent.

» *P. semiovatus* FRIES (LUNDELL)

Cap: 3–6 (9) cm broad by 2–6 cm high. Obtusely conic to parabolic at first, expanding to nearly convex. Cinnamon buff in young fruiting bodies becoming pinkish buff and fading in age to whitish. Surface viscid when moist, smooth to wrinkled. Flesh relatively thick, soft, and whitish.

Gills: Attachment adnexed and soon seceding from the stem, close to subdistant. Color pallid to brownish and eventually mottled blackish from the uneven ripening of the spores.

Stem: (8) 10–16 (18) cm long by (4) 6–10 (12) mm thick. Equal to slightly enlarged at the base; solid becoming tubular, and stuffed with a fibrous whitish pith. Whitish to pallid buff. Surface striate to smooth and powdered. Partial veil leaving a fragile membranous white annulus radially striate from the gills, and soon darkened by spores.

Growth habit and habitat: Solitary to scattered on dung in the spring and fall. Widely distributed throughout North America.

Comments: There has been conflicting reports on the edibility of this species. One collection analyzed contained psilocybin. This species is distinguished by the membranous annulus, the viscid cap, and its relatively large size. See also *P. phalaenarum.*

Microscopic characters: Spores 18.5–21.0 x 10–11.5 μ. Basidia 4-spored. Cheilocystidia absent. Pleurocystidia present, of the chrysocystidia type.

» *P. sp.*

Cap: 2–5 cm broad. Dark chestnut in young moist specimens, then becoming more yellowish brown, finally pallid grayish brown or tan when dry, sometimes with slight olive tones; yellowish brown. Nearly parabolic at first, then campanulate, convex to broadly convex in age. Margin initially incurved and undulated, soon straightening, and drying initially with a dark zone along its edge. Surface smooth, dry or only moist in wet conditions. Flesh pallid and relatively thick.

Gills: Attachment adnexed (ascending), soon seceding, and appearing free. Crowded, moderately broad, with three tiers of intermediate gills inserted. Dark purple-gray brown at maturity.

Stem: 4–10 cm long by 7–15 mm thick. Equal to slightly curved at the base and often enlarged towards the apex. Soon tubular. Nearly concolorous with the cap, covered with fine fibrils and dingy brown where touched. Surface dry, longitudinally striate at the apex, and finely fibrillose to pruinose. Partial veil finely cortinate or absent. Often bruising bluish at the base of the stem.

Growth habit and habitat: Typically growing gregariously to subcespitosely in the spring and fall on dung. Collected in northern California.

Comments: A presently unnamed species. It is often collected with *P. subbalteatus* and is similar. Hallucinogenic. Analysis has shown psilocybin, psilocin, and serotonin to be present.

Microscopic characters: Spores (10) 12–14 (15) x (6) 8–9 (10) μ. Pleurocystidia absent. Cheilocystidia present.

» *P. sphinctrinus* FRIES

Cap: 1.5–3 cm broad. Obtusely conic to campanulate. Grayish brown to reddish chestnut brown. Hygrophanous. Margin appendiculate, decorated with whitish, fragile, toothlike remnants of the partial veil. Surface moist or lubricous when very wet but soon dry. Flesh relatively thin to moderately thick, and nearly concolorous with the cap.

Gills: Attachment adnate to adnexed, crowded, and thin. Color dark grayish black and mottled from the uneven ripening of the spores.

Stem: 5–7.5 cm long by 2–4 mm thick. Equal, straight, firm, but hollow. Grayish brown with the context being a dark reddish purple. Surface pruinose with a grayish covering of fine fibrils.

Growth habit and habitat: Solitary to scattered on dung in the spring and fall. Widely distributed.

Comments: Rarely psilocybian. *P. sphinctrinus* and *P. campanulatus* comprise a tightly knit complex, and are almost inseparable. See also *P. papilionaceus.*

Microscopic characters: Spores 14.5–18.5 x 10.5–12.5 μ. Basidia 4- and rarely 2-spored. Cheilocystidia present. Pleurocystidia absent.

» *P. subbalteatus* BERKELEY AND BROOME

Cap: 4–5 cm broad at maturity. Convex to campanulate, then broadly convex, finally expanding to nearly plane with a broad umbo. Cinnamon brown to orange-cinnamon brown, fading to tan in drying with a dark brown encircling zone around the margin.

Stem: 5–6 cm long by 4 mm thick. Brittle, hollow, and fibrous. Reddish beneath minute whitish fibrils, darkening downwards. Oftentimes bruising bluish at the base.

Gills: Attachment adnate to uncinate, close, slightly swollen in the center, and with three tiers of intermediate gills inserted. Color brownish and mottled, with the edges remaining whitish, blackish when fully mature.

Growth habit and habitat: Growing cespitosely to gregariously in dung or in well manured ground in the spring, summer, and early fall. Reported from western North America and from the eastern United States.

Comments: Hallucinogenic. The cap and stem may bruise bluish green over a long period of time. Other panaeoli developing a dark band along the margin are *P. acuminatus, P. fimicola, P. foenisecii,* and *P. rickenii. P. subbalteatus* is also somewhat similar to *Panaeolus sp.* It is widely cultivated. The fact that the cap expands to plane with age is taxonomically significant.

Microscopic characters: Spores 11.5–14.0 x 7.5–9.5 μ. Basidia 2- and 4-spored. Cheilocystidia present. Pleurocystidia absent.

» *P. tropicalis* OLA'H

Cap: 1.5–2 (2.5) cm broad. Hemispheric

to convex to campanulate. Margin incurved at first, may elevate slightly with age, and not strongly translucent-striate unless very wet. Pallid or grayish to yellowish brown towards the disc, hygrophanous, often developing a marginal zone, bluish green in patches. Surface smooth to wrinkled, especially near the margin, and viscid when very wet.

Gills: Attachment adnexed to more or less uncinate, subdistant, with several tiers of intermediate gills. Distinctly mottled, dull grayish with dark blackish spotted areas.

Stem: 6–8 (12) cm long by 2–3 mm thick. Equal to swollen at the base, hollow. Grayish towards the apex, grayish brown in the middle area, and more blackish towards the base. Readily bruising bluish when touched. Surface longitudinally striate overall and pruinose towards the base. Partial veil absent.

Growth habit and habitat: Growing in cow dung and in the dung of wild animals in the tropics. Reported from Hawaii, and from southern California.

Comments: Contains psilocybin and/or psilocin. A very potent species for its size. See also *P. cyanescens.*

Microscopic characters: According to Ola'h (1969), the spores are internally granulated, measuring 10–12 x 7–9 μ. Basidia 2- or 4-spored. Cheilocystidia present 18–20–30 x 8–10 μ. Pleurocystidia present, 45–55 (60) x 10–13 (14) μ.

5 | Mushroom Cultivation

To AMATEUR mycologists, few experiences can match the excitement of cultivating mushrooms for the first time. The actual process for culturing mushrooms is relatively simple, though it demands considerable time and dedication on behalf of the cultivator. By far the greatest hindrance to successfully growing mushrooms is contamination by other fungi and bacteria. If one can effectively eliminate the presence of these contaminants and provide an adequately enriched and controlled environment, success in mushroom cultivation is practically assured.

Not all mushroom species will fruit outside their natural environment, but a great number of hallucinogenic and edible species can be grown under artificial conditions. Of these, *Psilocybe cubensis* has been the most popular psilocybian mushroom to cultivate. It can be fruited on a variety of substrates and is easily grown, as with most dung inhabiting psilocybes and panaeoli. *Panaeolus cyancescens* can be grown just as readily as *Psilocybe cubensis* and is highly prized for its potency and its comparatively small size. Recent experimentation with *Psilocybe cyanescens* has proven it can be fruited artificially on a mixture of wood chips and composted manure. In the wild, this species normally grows in a substrate of decomposed wood debris, like may psilocybes indigenous to North America. Employing the techniques described below (in some cases with minor modifications), many of the choice edible species can also be fruited in culture (*Agaricus bisporus, Pleurotus ostreatus,* possibly *Stropharia rugoso-annulata,* and others). Since several different methods for growing mushrooms are explored, read through the entire chapter before deciding upon any one technique.

Probably the simplest method for fruiting mushrooms involves spreading a great deal of spores of the desired species on a small quantity of composted manure, following the instructions for preparing compost on page 126. Place the finished compost in quart jars, autoclave in a pressure cooker for 45 minutes to an hour at 15 psi, and then allow to slowly return to atmospheric. Take the jars out of the pressure cooker. Upon cooling to nearly room temperature, remove the upside down lids and inoculate each jar with an ample quantity of spores (one spore print to four jars). If you have enough spores, try ten jars on the first run. Replace the lids loosely and set in a warm place. Every four or five days, lightly mist with a plant atomizer. Within two weeks, if the experiment has succeeded, whitish closely matted web-like growths should appear in the compost of at least several of these jars. Use each jar of *spawn* to inoculate larger volumes of compost. To fruit the cultures, follow the procedures outlined in the compost section of this chapter.

The most traditional method for fruiting mushrooms begins with the germination of spores on an enriched agar medium, growing out and isolating a pure culture, transferring the *mycelium* to autoclaved grain, all the while using *sterile technique*. The cultures can then be allowed to fruit on grain or they can be transferred and fruited on a manure compost (in combination with straw, wood chips, etc.). Throughout this entire process, contamination should be removed and destroyed as soon as it appears.

Agar

There are millions of air-borne particles such as spores floating around in the air we breathe, and from a practical point of view not much can be done to totally eliminate their presence. These foreign spores contaminate the mushroom cultures, causing the growth of highly competitive organisms (molds, some bacteria, etc.) which inhibit or prevent the growth of the desired mushroom mycelium. However, their movement is reduced and therefore the probability of contamination is lessened in still-air situations. When conducting these delicate transfers onto or from nutrient agar media, work in the most asceptic conditions possible. Spray your working areas with Lysol or a similar disinfectant, wash the inoculating table with soap and water, and then sponge with isopranol. (This is commonly known as rubbing alcohol. Be careful—alcohol can take off the finish of wood tables.) Since our very breath contains multitudes of unwanted microorganisms, you must be careful not to breathe over the sterilized areas during critical stages of the inoculating process.

You will need at least a dozen Petri dishes. The plastic ones initially come in a sterile state when purchased and can only be used once. Glass Petri dishes can be reused many times but are more costly at first. If you cannot get Petri dishes, any small glass containers—baby food jars, small Mason jars, etc.—can be used, though they are not as suitable. Make sure that whatever container you're using is sterile before pouring the agar media into it. The glassware can be made sterile by autoclaving in a pressure cooker at 15 psi for 30 minutes.

The basic agar media used for culturing mushroom mycelia has been PDY (Potato Dextrose Yeast) or MEA (Malt Extract Agar). Recently I have been introduced to a simplified formula for an agar medium ideal for mushroom mycelium. It is called Bob's Malt Medium.

Bob's Malt Medium
20 gm malt
20 gm agar
10 gm cornsteep fermentives
.2 gm $Ca(OH)_2$
.1 gm K_2HPO_4
1 l water

Bring 1 liter of water to boil. Add the ingredients. Continue to heat until everything is dissolved. Pour this liquid solution into a large glass flask and plug with cotton. Autoclave in a pressure cooker for 25 minutes at a pressure no greater than 10 psi or 240 degrees. Remove and allow the pressure to return to atmospheric, removing the flask. Let the flask cool for a few minutes and then quickly pour the liquid agar media into the Petri dishes. Culture tubes or test tubes stopped with cotton can be filled one-quarter full, angled at approximately 20 degrees, and allowed to solidify. These are called *slants* and are used for keeping stock cultures for long periods of time. As soon as the agar has cooled, the inoculation can begin.

There are two ways to acquire a culture of any mushroom species. The preferable method is to take tissue from fresh specimens; the other is to germinate spores. Since the entire mushroom is composed of compressed mycelia, a viable culture can be obtained from the cap flesh. Wipe the grit and pellicle (if present) off with a cotton swab dampened in alcohol. Dip the scalpel blade into alcohol or liquid Lysol and light it with an alcohol lamp. Continue to heat the tip until it is red hot. After allowing a few seconds to cool, scrape the surface of the cap, removing the uppermost layer of tissue, the pileal cuticle. Resterilize the blade in the above fashion and carefully cut more deeply into the flesh, removing a small fragment of tissue; quickly transfer it to a Petri dish. When making transfers, try to do it as quickly as possible, exposing the tissue and the agar for just a few seconds. Resterilize the blade, cool, and repeat this technique using several dishes. Label each dish with the date, species, type of agar, and any other pertinent data. For germinating spores, the technique is essentially the same but allow a few more seconds for the blade to cool down before touching the spores. Incubate the cultures at 75–85 degrees F for tropical species and 60–70 degrees F for temperate species.

Within several days a variety of growths will appear on the agar medium. It is not unusual for there to be contaminants at this stage. The presence of contaminants depends upon the way in which the inoculation was conducted, the quality of the spores or tissue transferred, and the sterility of the agar-filled containers. Mushroom mycelium is generally a whitish closely-matted or fuzzy web-like growth, though it can be quite different in appearance from one species to the next (see Fig. 53).

Using the sterile technique described previously, selectively transfer spots of mycelium to more agar plates with a scalpel. Repeat this process through as many generations as necessary until only pure cultures remain. Immediately seal all contaminated cultures in plastic and remove from the culturing area. After a pure culture has been established, transfer some mycelium into several stock culture tubes. After a week or two, store in a refrigerator. Stock cultures can be kept for a year, sometimes longer, and still be viable, provided the temperature does not drop below or approach freezing. In general, it is wise to transfer stock cultures every six months or to begin new ones. As a rule, no culture will remain uncontaminated or viable indefinitely. Stock cultures are your insurance against the possibility of contamination spreading throughout the other experiments, causing loss of the strain entirely.

Though some species can be induced to fruit on enriched agar, it is not a very effective or productive means of cultivation. Allow the mycelium to grow out over the entire surface of the agar before preparing for the next stage in the cultivation process. At this point you have basically two alternatives: to go onto grain or to go directly onto compost. Each has its advantages and disadvantages. The mushrooms will fruit quite well on grain, but with this medium contamination can be more of a problem. (Once pure grain cultures have been established, you could use them to inoculate compost.) The advantage of compost is that the mushrooms grown on it are usually much larger, contamination or properly composted manure is less of a problem, and many more mushrooms can be grown for the amount of time spent nursing them. Although grain does not require the special attention needed to correctly prepare compost, the greater likelihood of contamination can be avoided entirely by inoculating compost directly from agar plates much in the same way described for placing spores in Mason jars of autoclaved manure. If you do choose this method, it is

FIG. 51. Pressure cooker.   FIG. 52. Alcohol lamp and agar knife (scalpel).

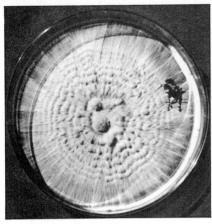

Fig. 53. Mycelium on agar.

Fig. 54. *Psilocybe cubensis* fruiting on agar.

recommended to pour a thin layer of agar within the Petri dishes and wait for the mycelium to permeate throughout the medium, leaving little or no surfaces exposed for contamination.

Grain

Many kinds of grain can be used to grow mushroom mycelium. The standard grain is rye, though rice, wheat, alfalfa, and even birdseed are sufficient for our purposes. The basic proportions for working with rye are described below. You can extrapolate from them if you wish to work with other grains.

Start out with a dozen Mason quart jars filled one-quarter full of rye with one-and-one-quarter times as much water in volume as grain. Invert the lids of each jar and loosely tighten their rims. Place the jars in a pressure cooker that is filled with ½ to 1 inch of water. (You may have to do several runs to autoclave all twelve jars.) Turn the burner on high heat and wait until there is a good head of steam coming through the open stop-cock. Close the valve and let the pressure rise to nearly 15 psi or 250 degrees. Maintain this pressure by adjusting the heat. After 45 minutes to an hour, the jars should be completely sterilized. Be very careful when leaving the pressure cooker unattended, as it can explode, especially if the cooker is not equipped with a safety valve. After nearly an hour, turn off the stove and wait for the pressure to come down to less than 5 psi; then start a slow leak. When the pressure is at atmospheric, the pressure cooker can be opened. Gently tighten the lids of the quart jars and check each one for cracks. Then shake each jar vigoroulsy to loosen up the grain which has nearly doubled in size. Place the jars in your inoculation area. After two hours they should be near room temperature.

Using sterile technique (spraying your area with a disinfectant, dipping scalpel in alcohol, flaming it over an alcohol lamp, etc.), transfer a portion of viable

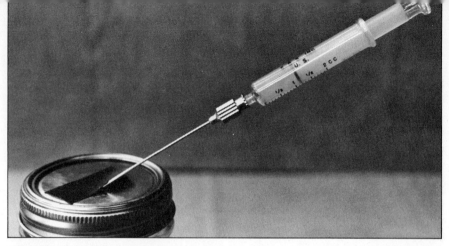

Fig. 55. Syringe inoculation of grain jars.

mycelium from a pure culture to each jar, lifting the lid for as short a time as possible. Throughout this entire procedure be very careful of your breathing and the speed in which the transfers are made. Repeat this tecnhique, transferring mycelium into all twelve jars. Store the cultures in a warm place and leave undisturbed for several days. In a few days, the mycelium will grow off the agar onto the kernels of grain. On the fourth to sixth day, shake the jars thoroughly to distribute the mycelium more evenly throughout the culture. In ten days or less the jars should be totally grown through with fuzzy whitish mushroom mycelium. If you wish, future inoculations onto grain can be made from these cultures, *if* they show no sign of contamination. Immediately kill any jar becoming contaminated by autoclaving in a pressure cooker.

Another method for inoculating rye grain in jars involves the use of the hypodermic syringe. It is by far the best technique for inducing rapid growth of mycelium through grain. Use a 5–10 ml syringe (where legal). Follow the same procedure for preparing the jars except punch a small 1 mm diameter hole in the top of each inverted lid. After autoclaving immediately cover these holes with tape while the jars are still hot. In this same run sterilize at least 200 ml of water in a flask stopped with cotton. When both water and grain have returned to room temperature, the inoculation can proceed.

Only absolutely pure cultures from Petri dishes or slants can be used for this technique. Otherwise, many other contaminants would become immersed in the water and contaminate the grain. Using an alcohol lamp, flame the needle until it is red hot. After a few seconds of cooling, draw 5–10 ml of sterilized water into the syringe. Carefully lift the edge of the Petri dish and squirt water on the mycelium covered agar. Redraw another 5–10 ml and repeat until the culture is completely submerged in water. This will largely depend upon the size of the Petri dish and the capacity of the syringe you are using. Then draw as many milliliters as possible from inside the dish while scraping the agar's surface, breaking up the mycelial mat. Suspended in the water of the syringe will be hundreds of minute fragments of mycelium. Inoculate a waiting rye grain jar, lifting up the tape and pushing the needle through the hole you made earlier. Squirt the water onto the grain. Repeat, using 15–20 ml of water/mycelium solution for every jar, and immediately replace the tape over the holes following inoculation. When choosing a syringe, try to get a large diameter needle so clogging will not be a problem. Between each inoculation re-sterilize the needle. Each Petri dish full of mycelium can inoculate from five to ten jars of grain. After finishing, drain off the excess water from the agar plates and store for future inoculations. In a few days, the mycelium will recover, and often fruitng will occur right in the dishes (with *Psilocybe cubensis, Panaeolus cyanescens,* and *Panaeolus subbalteatus.*)

In five to ten days, the mycelium will permeate throughout the jars. You may shake them if you want, but this should not be necessary. The probability of contamination is greatly reduced using the syringe technique, and the extra water may encourage an earlier fruiting.

After the jars have been totally run through with mycelium, they can be used to inoculate compost, dug out into cake dishes to maximize surface area for fruiting, or cased as they are and allowed to fruit. If you dig out the jars into dishes, use sterile conditions. Spread mycelium covered grain in a two inch layer on the bottom of a clean cake dish, casserole bowl, or similar utensil. Glass is preferable. Cover the containers with plastic. In a few days, the mycelium will become fuzzy again and after a week the cultures can be cased. Even though the surface area is increased and the number of aborts seems reduced, it is not certain whether this method in the end increases mushroom production.

The casing is a rich light soil applied to the cultures to encourage fruiting. It is definitely recommended to sterilize the casing before application. This layer of soil seems to act as an interphase between the mycelium and the water, helping to retain an overall moisture content within the culture and to some extent supporting the mushrooms as they fruit. It should always be kept moist once the mushroom mycelium has shown signs of growing up into it. Apply an even ½ to 1 inch layer of casing soil using the formula described below.

Fig. 56. Mycelium on agar with primordia.

Fig. 57. *Psilocybe cubensis* fruiting on grain (Leslie strain 1902).

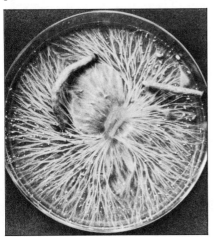

Casing
3½ parts peat moss
2   parts vermiculite or perlite
2   parts fine sand
2   parts crushed oyster shell

After casing the jars or dishes, spray the cultures once or twice in the first week to encourage mycelial growth into the soil. During this time, keep the cultures covered, either with the lids inverted but loosely tightened for jars or with plastic over the dishes. On the tenth day after casing, begin a daily watering schedule. Keep the soil moist but not soggy. Soon, primordia will form. These are small white dots, growing in the matter of days into fully mature mushrooms.

Compost

When circumstances permit, one can successfully cultivate many mushrooms on a composted straw–manure medium. Cultivation on manure becomes a much larger scale operation than with grain, one which would be difficult to conduct in the kitchen of your home. For this reason, and because the preparation of the dung and straw is critically important, many people prefer to cultivate only on grain. However, by following the recipe described below, a large quantity of mushrooms can be grown.

Straw–Manure Medium
1 pick-up load of leached cow manure or fresh horse manure
2 bales of wheat straw
25 pounds of horticultural gypsum (not lime)
2 packages (5 lbs. apiece) compost starter
5 pounds cottonseed meal

Horse stables often sell a rich mixture of manure and straw from their stables, which can be perfect for mushroom cultivation. The further addition of straw to this mixture is not necessary. Try to get the straw–manure within a day or two after being removed from the stables. Discard any material having whitish growths running through it as this means another fungus has already taken control. The presence of *Coprinus niveus*, the most common of wild species to invade manure, usually indicates under-composting. As the compost matures, this species recedes, becoming less of a competitor.

Wheat straw is commonly available at feed stores. Gypsum powder, and cottonseed meal can be found at most gardening stores. Leached manure for the compost can be bought from large dairies that use a process of washing all cow wastes in a large vat separating the solids from the liquids. The liquid wastes are then spread over the fields as a fertilizer; the remaining coarser material is perfect for mushroom cultivation. Not all dairies use this process, and some know nothing about it. The going price for a truckload of leached manure is usually under ten dollars. If you are unsuccessful in your search for a dairy that has this type of manure, try making your own by putting fairly fresh manure on a half-inch meshed screen, washing the manure thoroughly with a hose, and retaining the coarser residual material for mushroom compost.

Open the bales of straw, stack it in a heap, and soak it thoroughly with water. Rinse the heap several times over the course of two or three days. Meanwhile, make a separate pile for compost by stacking manure in a layer 10–12 inches in depth over a four-by-six-foot square area. Fluff the soaked straw with a pitchfork and place one third of it as a layer over the manure. Sprinkle this straw liberally with gypsum and cottonseed meal. Wash the straw layer with water to carry these ingredients into the manure. Repeat this layering process two times; you should get a pile about four feet high. Generally, the higher the pile the better. Let the compost sit for a week to ten days. During this time keep a close watch on how well the pile is heating up. Sometimes, compost piles have caught on fire from the excessive heat generated within them. In a short while the temperature of the pile will gradually rise, reaching 140 or 160 degrees F, especially towards the center, and remaining there for several days.

After seven to ten days, the center of the pile should be completely composted. Peel off the outside layers and take out the center. Reconstruct the pile. Finished compost will be darker than unfinished material, and the straw should be more brownish than yellowish. Discard any material that smells of ammonia. Place the finished compost into boxes lined with plastic garbage bags to a depth of 10 or 12 inches. Be sure to thoroughly mix together the extracted compost as some parts of it will be more done than others. As you transfer the composted straw to the boxes, it should feel hot to the touch.

In a day or two, the compost in the boxes will have cooled to 80 or 85 degrees. Sometimes, secondary fermentation occurs, raising the temperature to 110 degrees or higher. This would kill most mushroom mycelium. When the boxes have cooled to nearly room temperature, dig out six four-inch diameter holes in the compost of each box. Plug every hole with mycelium-covered rye grain. Cover the holes with an inch or two of compost. If you do not have enough grain cultures to inoculate all the boxes, do as many boxes as possible, and then use these to inoculate other boxes once the mycelium has grown through it.

Spray the cultures once a day with a plant atomizer or with a hose equipped with a half-gallon per minute mist attachment with an on/off valve. In ten days, the mycelium should be through much of the compost. At this stage, a one inch casing of soil can be applied. This is not essential; fruiting will occur without it. Experience with *Agaricus bisporus* has shown that casing greatly increases the yield, but I do not know if this is true for *Psilocybe cubensis* and other species. If you apply a casing, follow the formula described on page 126.

At about the time of casing, the second turning of the compost should be undertaken. Follow the same procedure as in the first turn. You can expect at least three turns of the pile before totally depleting it. By the third turn of the pile, the fruiting of the first turn should be well underway.

FIG. 58. *Psilocybe cubensis* on compost.

Whether you choose to cultivate on grain or compost, the role of temperature and humidity should be carefully considered. If the temperature is near natural for the species cultivated, fruiting should be maximixed. A 30 degree F day-to-night fluctuation in temperature is probably not inhibiting—it may even be beneficial—but any greater variation has generally shown to be counter-productive. Equally important as temperature is humidity. The ideal conditions for mushroom cultivation is a system that is high in humidity but has an occasional flow of fresh air. If you can design such a system, and maintain an ideal temperature, the mushrooms need only light to fruit. (The steam vaporizers that are sold to 'soothe a child's sore throat while sleeping' are very good for creating such a system.)

The function light plays in the life cycle of many mushrooms is important. Though mushrooms are non-photosynthetic, many need light and often orient themselves to it as they grow. Indirect natural light seems perfect, though florescent light also works well.

Spray the mushrooms as they fruit from a distance of about twelve inches.

There are many ways to cultivate mushrooms and by varying the experiments, you will arrive at the best formula. Limits exist for fruiting mushrooms artificially, but these tend to vary according to a species' individual nature and are often obscure, leaving a great deal of latitude for imaginative experimentation.

Selected Bibliography for Mushroom Cultivation

Ames, R., Singer, R., Smith, A.H., and Stein, S.I. 1959. "Agarics Causing Cerebral Mycetisms, Part II. The Influence of Temperature on Mycelial Growth of *Psilocybe, Panaeolus,* and *Copelandia.*" *Mycopathologia et Mycologia Applicata* 9:268–275.

Atkins, F.C. 1966. *Mushroom Growing To-day.* New York: MacMillan Publishing Co.

Burrows, W. 1968. *Textbook of Microbiology.* Philadelphia: Saunders.

Enos, L. 1970. *A Key to the North American Psilocybin Mushrooms.* Lemon Grove, Calif.: Youniverse Productions.

Genders, R. 1969. *Mushroom Growing for Everyone.* New York: MacMillan Publishing Co.

Harris, B. 1976. *Growing Wild Mushrooms.* Berkeley: Wingbow Press.

Kneebone, L.R. 1960. "Hallucinogenic Fungi." *Developments in Industrial Microbiology* 1:109.

Oss, O.T., and Oeric, O.N. 1976. *Psilocybin Magic Mushroom Grower's Guide.* Berkeley: And/Or Press.

Pinkerton, M.H. 1954. *Commercial Mushroom Growing.* Ernst Benn Ltd.

Pollock, S.H. 1977. *Magic Mushroom Cultivation.* San Antonio: Herbal Medicine Research Foundation.

Robinson, W. 1870. *Mushroom Culture—Its Extension and Improvement.* Philadelphia: Frederick Warne and Co.

Rodale, J.I., and staff. 1975. *The Complete Book of Composting.* Emmaus, Pa.: Rodale Books, Inc.

San Antonio, J.P. 1971. "A Laboratory Method to Obtain Fruit from Cased Grain Spawn of the Cultivated Mushroom, *Agaricus bisporous*." *Mycologia* 63:16–21.

Singer, R. 1958. "Mycological Investigations on *Teonanácatl,* the Mexican Hallucinogenic Mushroom, Part I." *Mycologia* 50:239–256.

FIG. 59. Mycelium on compost.

FIG. 60. *Psilocybe cyanescens* on wood chips.

APPENDIX 1

The Mushroom Life Cycle

GILLED mushrooms are one of the most specialized forms of fleshy fungi. The spores are produced on the gill surface by a cell called a *basidium*. This usually has four spores, though several mushroom species have basidia with as few as two and as many as eight. (*Agaricus bisporus*, the common store-bought variety, has 2-spored basidia while the well-known chantarelle, *Cantharellus cibarius*, has 6-, 7-, and 8-spored basidia!)

The Strophariaceae and Coprinaceae species have spores that are typically ellipsoid with a *hilar appendage* (or 'nipple') at one end and a depressed *pore* at the other (see Fig. 61 and Diagram E, No. 1). This same general spore shape is also characteristic of other genera, such as *Conocybe* and *Lepiota*. It is through these spores that fungi reproduce and propagate. In the ensuing text, the mushroom life cycle is fully described, illustrated with Diagram E and scanning electron micrographs (Figs. 61–75).

The mushroom fruiting body or *basidiocarp* represents but a small portion of the entire life cycle of the mycelium, the actual fungal plant. The mycelium is composed of many individual cells called *hyphae* by which the plant grows through a series of cellular (mitotic) divisions and fusions. The life cycle of the agarics is a continuous process, best viewed microscopically beginning at the stage where the spores have already been projected into the atmosphere.

Spores are the reproductive bodies or 'seeds' of fungi. In some species and under the proper environmental conditions, the spore germinates from the germ pore into a strand of hypha (see Fig. 62, 63 and Diagram E, No. 2). This hyphal strand is haploid and mononucleate in its chromosomal composition, meaning that in each cell there is one nucleus containing one half of the full number of chromosomes (1N) of the particular mushroom species. The spores and their subsequent hyphae are sexual (+ and −) in their reproductive nature to the extent

The Mushroom Life Cycle

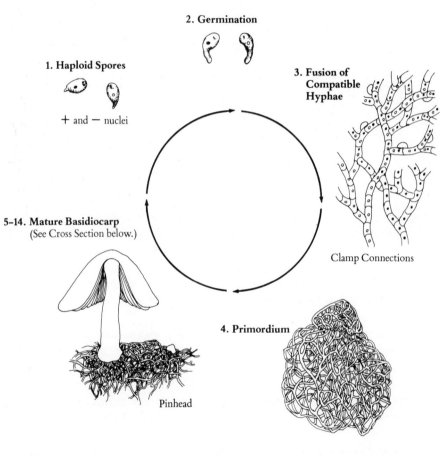

2. Germination

1. Haploid Spores

+ and − nuclei

3. Fusion of Compatible Hyphae

Clamp Connections

5–14. Mature Basidiocarp
(See Cross Section below.)

4. Primordium

Pinhead

CROSS SECTION OF GILL

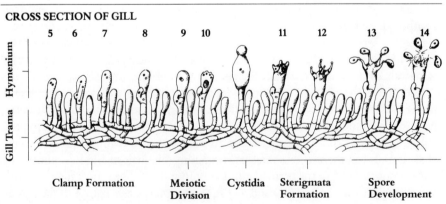

| | 5 | 6 | 7 | 8 | 9 | 10 | | 11 | 12 | | 13 | 14 |

Hymenium — Gill Trama

Clamp Formation   Meiotic Division   Cystidia   Sterigmata Formation   Spore Development

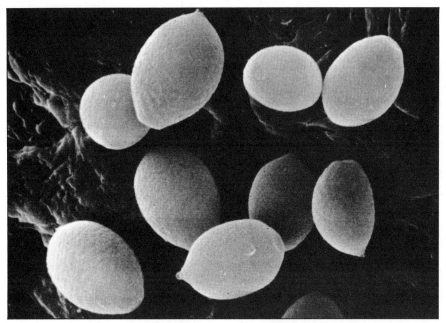

FIG. 61. *Panaeolus castaneifolius* spores.

that only compatible hyphal strands will fuse. The two compatible cells which are mononucleate coelesce to form a single cell that has two separate + and − nuclei (see Diagram E, No. 3).

The nuclei remain independent of one another at this stage and the new type of cell can be described as being *haploid* and *binucleate* (1N, 1N.). Haploid binucleate cells contain two nuclei, each of which still has half the total number of chromosomes for the particular species. These cells continue to reproduce mitotically and for many species this nuclear division occurs by means of a clamp connection. These connections form at the cross walls or junction of the two haploid and binucleate, or dikaryotic, cells (see Fig. 64). The presence or absence of these clamp connections can be taxonomically significant for distinguishing species. They can be seen on the hyphae or just beneath the basidia. Clamp connections play an essential role in the development of the basidia and the growth of the mushroom hyphae. They can be found only between binucleate cells during the dikaryophase. Hyphae grow into a dense mat known as mycelium. At some point during this phase, the mycelium becomes stimulated through an unknown biological mechanism (light seems to play an important role with many psilocybian species) and rapidly grows, amassing in dense forms called 'pinheads' or *primordia*. These further develop to produce the mature mushrooms (see Fig. 65 and Diagram E, No. 4). The formation of primordia always follows the occurence of clamp connections or the dikaryophase.

As the primordia enlarge and differentiate, the various structures of the mushroom quickly take shape. The stem elevates the cap above ground so spores

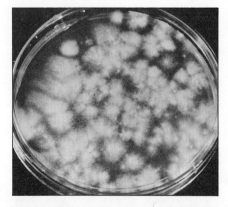

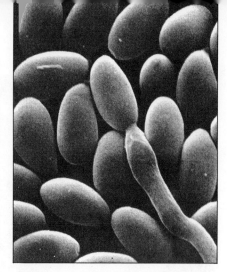

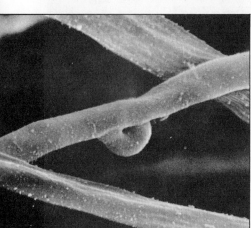

Fig. 62. Spore germination on agar.

Fig. 63. Spore germination of *Psilocybe baeocystis.*

Fig. 64. Clamp connection of *Psilocybe cubensis.*

Fig. 65. Primordium (mushroom pinhead) of *Psilocybe cubensis.*

Fig. 66. Hymenium and gill trama of *Panaeolus foenisecii.*

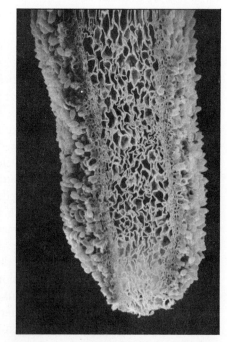

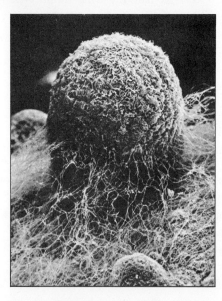

can be released freely into the air. It also acts as a conduit of nutrients for the rest of the plant. The function of the cap is to act as a domed shield protecting the maturing gills underneath. Both cap and stem cells remain in the dikaryotic state for the rest of the life cycle. During this time, the cells on the gill surface are undergoing rapid differentiation as the fruiting body matures.

The gill is composed of two basic layers of tissue. The fertile cell bearing layer which eventually grows the spores is called the *hymenium*. It is usually only a few cells thick, comparatively thinner than the underlying tissue of the gill trama. The cells of the hymenium essentially extend out of the gill trama. For taxonomists, the arrangement of the interwoven strands of hyphae can be important for separating species (see Fig. 66).

The immature gills are initially covered by a multitude of similar, low rounded cells called *basidioles* and *cystidioles.* As the mushroom matures, inflated cells arise from the hymenium. Basidioles may grow into the fertile spore bearing *basidia,* whereas cystidioles have potential to grow into non-sporulating sterile cells, *cystidia.* The cells are very distinct in their shape and function. With the species I have viewed under the scanning electron microscope, it appears that cystidia preceed the development of basidia from the hymenial layer.

The function of the cystidia is not well understood. They may have many purposes or possibly none at all, considering that a great number of mushroom species lack cystidia altogether. On the gill two types of cystidia can often be seen. Most all species of *Psilocybe* and *Panaeolus* have cystidia on the gill margins or edges, called *cheilocystidia,* which lend a whitish appearance on the margin. (This can be readily seen in the field.) When cystidia appear on the gill surface, they are

FIG. 67. Cheilocystidia of *Psilocybe baeocystis;* view of gill edge.

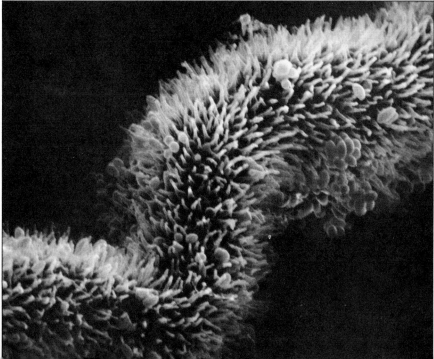

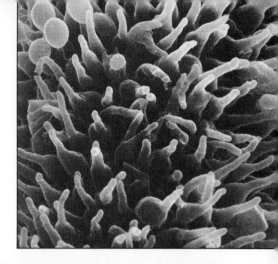

Fig. 68. Cheilocystidia of *Psilocybe baeocystis;* close up of Fig. 67.

Fig. 69. Gill surface of *Panaeolus foenisecii* showing gill edge and surface.

Fig. 70. Pleurocystidium of *Panaeolus cyanescens.*

Fig. 71. Pleurocystidia of *Psilocybe cubensis.*

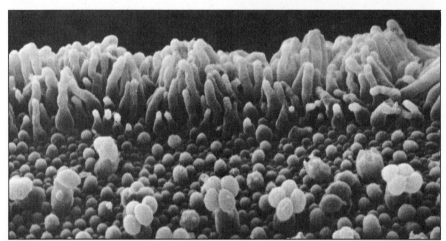

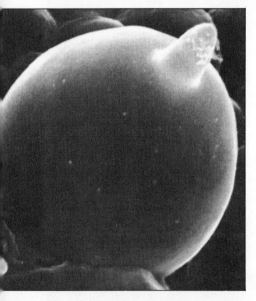

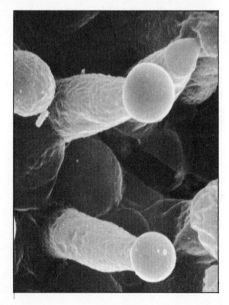

called *pleurocystidia*. Only a few species of *Psilocybe* and *Panaeolus* exhibit this feature, and its presence is a very good way to identify mushrooms microscopically (see Figs. 67–71).

One hypothesis on the function of cystidia is that they accumulate and store the metabolic waste products of the fruiting body during its active but short-lived period of existence. Another very plausible hypothesis suggests that cystidia, especially cheilocystidia with their massive surface areas, act to regulate relative humidity in spaces between the gills through moisture evaporation. The increased humidity would help insure maturity of the basidia and spores, and thus the survival of the species.

The vast majority of cells that populate the maturing gill surface are the basidia. Clamp connections soon appear on the basidioles while they are in the dikaryotic state (see Fig. 72 and Diagram E, No. 5). Soon afterwards, the two nuclei of each basidiole subdivide, replicating themselves mitotically, into four haploid (1N) nuclei (see Diagram E, No. 6). At this point, there are essentially two pairs of sexually opposite nuclei present in each cell. One of these four nuclei migrates into the cavity of the clamp (see Diagram E, No. 7). The clamp, which has always been pointed towards the base of the basidium, extends and a new cell wall forms, dividing the terminal portion of the basidium with its two nuclei from the nucleus at the opposite end. Almost simultaneously, the clamp has elongated far enough to touch the newly forming cell and another cell wall appears, isolating the clamp from the parent cell. When the apical end of the clamp touches the new cell, the two cells merge, becoming one and restoring the binucleate nature (see Diagram E, No. 8). From the lower cell, a new hyphal branch can grow and mitotic cellular division can take place in the manner described above.

Soon, the two haploid and sexually complementary nuclei of the terminal basidium come together to create a mononucleate and diploid (2N) nucleus. This

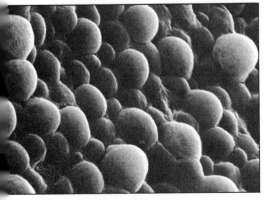

FIG. 72. Basidioles.

FIG. 73. Immature basidia (foreground) of *Panaeolus castaneifolius*.

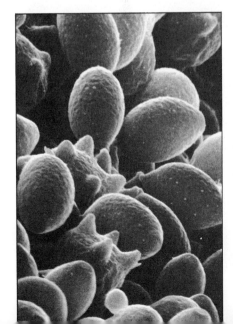

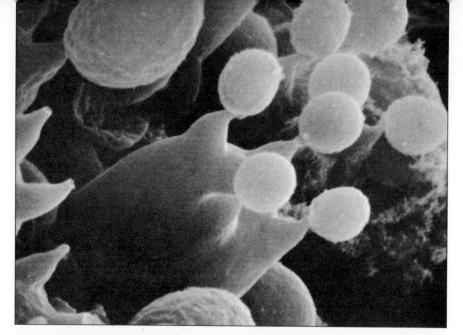

FIG. 74. Young basidia of *Panaeolus foenisecii* with developing spores.

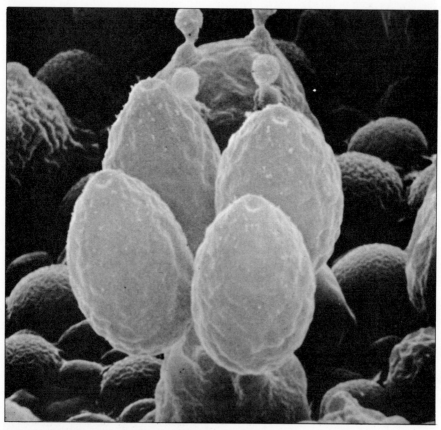

FIG. 75. Basidium of *Panaeolus foenisecii* at maturity.

is called *karyogamy* (see Diagram E, No. 9). Then, *meiosis* or reduction division occurs and four mononucleate haploid nuclei result (see Diagram E, No. 10). Meanwhile the fruiting body is rapidly growing, with the basidioles inflating, and with the partial veil in its initial states of stretching (based on observations of cultivated *Psilocybe cubensis*). This is the earliest phase of the formation of the spores. The many vacuoles within the cell of the basidium come together to make one huge vacuole which continues to enlarge, increasing cytoplasmic pressure in the direction of the cell apex. From four specific sites on the apical surface of the basidium, four *sterigmata* grow and elongate (see Fig. 73 and Diagram E, Nos. 11 and 12). The nuclei move to the tips of the sterigmata and the true basidiospores originate (see Diagram E, No. 13, Fig. 74). As soon as the spores mature, a *hilar appendage* develops at the spore–sterigmata junction and is arranged in such a way that the spores are directed outwards from one another (see Fig. 75). Upon maturity, a 'gas bubble' forms at this junction, rapidly inflates, and violently explodes, jettisoning the basidiospores into space (see Diagram E, No. 14). Essentially, this completes the life cycle.

APPENDIX 2

The Microscopic Dimension

PSILOCYBIAN mushrooms can be viewed from many different perspectives. One which most people are not familiar with exists in the microscopic realm. The invention of the light microscope provided a greater stimulus for biological sciences than any other instrument in the nineteenth century. Microscopes held much the same implications for biologists as telescopes did for the early astronomers. With both inventions, whole new worlds were revealed for the first time. Man's notions of reality and his awareness of the universe expanded immensely. The world was no longer a distance a ship could sail or a horizon seen from the highest mountain. Instead, reality became a vast spatial continuum, limitless in depth.

In the past decade, refinement of the technology behind scanning electron microscopes has furthered the capabilities ten-fold for viewing the microscopic world. Whereas light microscopes produce a two dimensional image in a shallow depth of field and are very limited in their magnifications capabilities (several thousand diameters at most), scanning electron microscopes give a three dimensional image of very high resolution with a remarkable depth of field, and can magnify specimens several hundred thousand diameters. With scanning electron microscopy, however, the specimens are killed in the preparation, while light microscopy allows the advantage of observing on-going life processes. Recently, electron microscopy has proven to be very useful for mycological studies.

Before a specimen can be placed into the scanning electron microscope, it has to be specially prepared. First, a fresh young mushroom is selected from a collection and fixed in osmium tetroxide which strengthens the carbon bonds, reinforcing the molecular structure of the mushroom cells. After a series of dehydration baths in alcohol, the specimen is submerged into liquid nitrogen for several seconds and then freeze fractured. This is followed by another series of acetone baths. Eventually the specimen is critically point dried, a process whereby biological material is dried without distorting the micro-structure of the cells. Finally, the specimens are plated with a very thin layer of gold. (This is only one method of specimen preparation; there are many.)

At this point the specimen is ready to be put into the scanning electron microscope, which shoots a fine electron beam at the mushroom in a high vacuum chamber. Two magnetic scan generators move the beam downward and across the specimen in a grid pattern. The entire surface area of the mushroom cross-section is scanned in only one-sixtieth of a second. As the beam hits the specimen, secondary electrons are reflected off its surface. These secondary electrons are picked up by a detector plate positioned above and to the side of the specimen. After going through a series of complicated electronic translators, an image is eventually produced and displayed on a television monitor. The image is brighter where there are more secondary electrons being emitted from the surface and hitting the detector plate, and conversely dimmer where there are fewer secondary electrons bouncing off the specimen's surface. In turn, magnification increases as the total surface area scanned by the electron beam decreases. Fundamentally this is the principle behind scanning electron microscopy.

When looking at mushrooms through the scanning electron microscope, particularly on the gill surface, a number of distinct kinds of cells can be seen. The scanning electron micrographs in Appendix 1 beautifully illustrate the mushroom life cycle in the growth of spores and development of their parent cells, the basidia. Knowing the life cycle of mushrooms, amateurs and those especially interested in cultivation can relate field observations and culturing techniques to actual phenomena occurring in the microscopic realm.

Basic Light Microscopy

At times, the addition of microscopic data is the advantage mushroom hunters need to positively identify the closest of related species. Light microscopy technique is essentially a very simple process when working with fresh material. Working from dried material is somewhat more involved (you must be sure the tissue is properly rehydrated), but still it is not difficult. After a few hours practice, you will soon have the necessary skills to identify mushrooms microscopically, and in most cases, definitively.

You will need a good light microscope with magnifying capacity of at least 400X and preferably 1000X with an oil-immersion lens. The eyepiece should be equipped with a calibrated micron bar, as measurements of spores, cystidia, and other microscopic parts are very important. The mushroom material must be mounted in a liquid solution before it can be viewed microscopically. The standard mounting solution is potassium hydroxide (KOH) dissolved in water at a concentration of 2½%, or 2½ grams of KOH to 97½ grams of distilled water (100 ml of H_2O weighs 100 g). Because 100 milliliters is quite a volume to be working with considering you will be using it a drop at a time, reduce the volume according to your needs. The mounting solution should be kept in a small bottle stopped with an eye dropper. Have glass microscope slides available and cover slips, preferably no. 0 or no. 1 thickness. Note that KOH is caustic and should be handled with care.

The techniques described in the following paragraphs are directed towards amateurs especially interested in identifying psilocybian and related species. They serve only as an introduction and as a means to convey necessary light microscopy techniques for people using this book. For descriptions of other micro-techiques, consult the texts listed in the Annotated Bibliography of General Mushroom Field Guides.

For the most part, there are four types of cells that can be very useful taxonomically in determining a species. They are the *spores, cheilocystidia, pleurocystidia* (including *chrysocystidia*), and cells composing the cap cuticle (or *epicutis*).

SPORES

The length and width of mushroom spores are often employed by taxonomists for separating species microscopically. Place a drop of 2½% KOH on a clean glass slide and with a scalpel scrape spores from a spore print. (It is best to measure spores on the stem because these will be truly mature and representative of the species.) Touch the scalpel tip containing the spores to the KOH droplet. Place the cover slip over it and press down using the eraser end of a pencil while absorbing the excess liquid with a cotton swab. At first the spores may appear agitated but should soon remain still. If there is excessive drifting, too much KOH solution remains between the cover slip and the microscope slide.

CHEILOCYSTIDIA

Since these sterile cells are positioned along the gill edge, they can be easily prepared for observation. Slice the mushroom in half with a razor blade and remove an entire gill, placing it on another glass slide especially set aside for this purpose. Carefully cut the *thinnest* section possible parallel to the gill margin. Try to do it so that the thin section, which should be barely discernible, remains on the edge of the razor blade. Draw the material from the razor edge onto a clean microscope slide by placing a drop of KOH at the point of contact between the blade and the glass. The gill material should flow into the droplet on the slide. Place a cover slip over it and draw off the excess liquid using a cotton swab. The specimen should then be ready for viewing.

PLEUROCYSTIDIA (AND CHRYSOCYSTIDIA)

The preparation of a good specimen for studying pleurocystidia demands more skill than for the previous two cells. Getting the thinnest cross-section possible is extremely important. Often pleurocystidia are not present in great numbers and since they exist on the surface of the gill, not on the edge like cheilocystidia, the plane of the slice has to intersect them in order for them to be seen. Some species which have been described by mycologists using light microscopes as having pleurocystidia 'few in numbers' or 'rarely seen' have appeared to abound with them when viewed through the scanning electron microscope. This is because the plane of cross sectioning often misses many of the surface cystidia.

There are two ways of thin sectioning a gill to find pleurocystidia. It is recommended to try the first and then go on to the second once you understand just what is needed. Follow the procedure described for cheilocystidia but instead of cutting out a small section along the gill, make a wider cut and remove the entire gill margin. In a perpendicular direction cut the gill in half, discarding one portion. (At this point it is a good idea to wipe the razor edge clean.) As with the cheilocystidia, cut the thinnest slice possible so the resulting gill tissue on the razor's edge is barely visible. Bring this thin section to a clean microscope slide and draw off the tissue with a drop of KOH. Place a cover slip over the specimen, soaking up the excess with a cotton swab.

The second method is better because several gills are sectioned simultaneously. Cut a wedge from the mushroom cap and, grasping it in hand with gills oriented vertically, cut in a horizontal fashion across the gill plates. Clean the razor edge and place a drop or two of KOH on its upper surface. With a smooth even movement of the wrist, slowly and carefully cut across the gill surfaces. As you cut the gills, pieces of tissue will be drawn up into the mounting solution. If the sectioning seems disproportionate, with some parts thicker than others, pick out and discard the thickest of them. Transfer the gill material to a microscope slide, place a cover slip on it, and press down with the eraser end of a pencil while soaking up excess KOH solution. If done well, you should have several gill cross sections from which the pleurocystidia, cheilocystidia, basidia, spores, and gill trama can be studied.

In all species of *Naematoloma* and most species of *Stropharia* there exists a special type of cystidia (mostly facial but sometimes marginal) called *chrysocystidia,* a cell that has a highly refractive yellowish brown mass within it. This cell can only be seen in dried material that has been revived in 2½% KOH. By definition of the genus, *Psilocybe* is without chrysocystidia, though it may possess other types of cystidia. The absence or presence of these types of cells, their shape, and the nature by which light diffuses through them aid in establishing a species identification.

THE CAP CUTICLE

This book has followed a certain interpretation of the families Strophariaceae and Coprinaceae. These families differ mostly by the nature of the cap cuticle, which is filamentous in *Naematoloma, Psilocybe,* and *Stropharia,* while cellular in *Coprinus, Panaeolus,* and *Psathyrella.* A filamentous epicutis is composed of long interwoven strands of hyphae and often undergoes partial gelatinization (causing the cap to feel viscid to the touch). A cellular cap cuticle is made up of globose or rounded cells which generally do not undergo gelatinization. Sometimes, as in *Panaeolus semiovatus,* a gelatinous layer of interwoven filaments rests upon a cellular cap cuticle. This is generally the exception, not the rule.

Using a razor, cut a cap in half and then slice a thin section (parallel to the first cut) from the very upper surface layer. Place the tissue on a slide with KOH and cover with a glass microscope slip. Disperse the cells by applying force with the eraser end of a pencil while soaking up the excess liquid.

If you have difficulty obtaining a good image through the microscope, the addition of vegetable dye to the KOH solution can help increase contrast. Measure at least twenty cells of each type, trying to get a representative sampling, and record their sizes and shapes. With field observations and precise microscopic information, mushroom identification becomes a highly certain process.

GLOSSARY

acute   Pointed, sharp.

adnate (of gills)   bluntly attached to the stem. See Diagram B.

adnexed (of gills)   Attached to the stem in an ascending manner. See Diagram B.

Agaricaceae   a family of mushrooms with primarily one genus, *Agaricus.*

Agaricales   The order which includes all mushrooms with true gills.

agarics   Mushrooms with gills.

amyloid   The characteristic bluish reaction the flesh or the spores of a mushroom exhibits in Melzer's iodine.

angstrom 10^{-10} meters, one tenth of a micron.

annular (on the stem)   Resembling a ring as in 'annular zone'. See Diagram C.

annulate   Having an annulus.

annulus   The tissue remnants of the partial veil adhering to the stem and forming a membranous ring. See Diagram C.

apex (of the stem)   The 'top' or highest point or region.

apiculus   The nipple-like projection by which the spore is attached to the sterigmata of the basidium.

appendiculate (of the cap margin)   Hanging with veil remnants.

appressed   Flattened.

ascending (of the gills)   Where the gills extend upwards from the margin of the cap to their attachment at the stem.

Ascomycetes   Fungi which produce spores by an ascus, a sac-like cell, as opposed to the basidium of Basidiomycetes.

attachment   The 'connection' between the gills and the stem.

atypical   Not typical.

autoclave   To steam-pressurize.

autonomous   Being of its own; an entity in itself.

Basidiomycetes   All fungi which bear spores upon a basidium, as opposed to the Ascomycetes which bear spores in an ascus.

basidia, basidium   A particular fertile cell in which meiosis occurs and by which spores are produced. See Appendix 1.

basidiocarp   The fruiting body that produces basidia.

binucleate   Having two nuclei in one cell.

broad A relative term connoting width (as opposed to length) in reference to the gills (in the order narrow, moderately broad, broad).

buff Dingy yellowish brown.

campanulate (of the cap) Bell-shaped. See Diagram A.

carpophore The mushroom fruiting body.

cartilaginous Brittle, not pliant.

caulocystidia Sterile cells on the stem.

cellular Composed of globose to generally rounded cells, not 'thread-like'.

cespitose Growing clustered from a common base.

cheilocystidia Sterile cells on the gill edge. Sometimes called 'marginal cystidia'.

chrysocystidia A type of cystidia that is highly refractive in once-dried tissue revived with a potassium hydroxide (KOH) solution. It appears as a yellowish brown amorphous mass within the cell.

clamp connection An 'elbow-like' protrubence which arches over the walls between cells in dikaryotic mycelium of some mushroom species. See Appendix 1.

close (of the gills) A relative term in reference to the spacing of the gills (in the order crowded, close, subdistant, distant).

complex A cluster of similarly related species typified by a central species.

concolorous Having the same color.

conic (of the cap) Shaped like a cone. See Diagram A.

context A term for the 'flesh' of the cap or stem.

convex (of the cap) See Diagram A.

Coprinaceae A family of mushrooms containing the genera *Coprinus, Panaeolus,* and *Psathryella.*

coprophilous Growing on dung.

cortinate A type of partial veil consisting of fine cobweb-like threads. See Diagram C.

crowded (of the gills) A relative term used in describing the narrow spacing of the gills (in the order crowded, close, subdistant, distant). See Diagram C.

cuspid Sharp, pointed.

cuticle The surface layer of cells on the cap that can undergo varying degrees of differentation.

cystidia Microscopic sterile cells.

decurrent (of the gills) The attachment where the gills markedly run down the stem.

deciduous Describing trees which seasonally shed their leaves.

decurved (of the margin) Where the shape or curvature bends directly downwards.

deliquescing The process of autodigestion by which the gills and cap melt into a liquid. Typical of the *Coprinus* genus and some species of the Bolbitiaceae family.

denticulate 'Tooth-like'.

dichotomous Repeatedly splitting or forking in pairs.

dikaryophase The phase in which there are two individual nuclei in each cell of the mushroom plant.

dikaryotic The state of cells in the dikaryophase.

diploid A genetic condition where each cell has a full set of chromosomes for the particular species (2N).

disc The central portion of the cap.

distant A relative term implying the broad spacing of the gills (in the order crowded, close, subdistant, distant). See Diagram C.

eccentric Off-centered.

elevated (of the margin) Describing the type of cap whose margin is uplifted, usually seen in age. See Diagram A.

ellipsoid Shaped like an oblong circle.

equal (of the stem) Evenly thick.

eroded (of the margin of the cap or the gills) Irregularly broken.

evanescent Fragile and soon disappearing.

fibrillose Having fibrils.

fibrils Fine, delicate 'hairs' found on the surface of the cap or stem.

fibrous (of the stem) Composed of tough, string-like tissue.

filamentous Composed of hyphae or 'thread-like' cells, which may undergo gelatinization.

flexuose, flexuous (of the stem) Bent alternately in opposite directions. See Diagram C.

floccose, flocculose Easily removed, usually referring to wooly tufts or cottony veil remnants on the cap or stem.

fugacious Impermanent, easily torn or destroyed.

fusoid (of the cystidia) Rounded and tapering from the center.

gelatinous Having the consistency of jelly.

glabrescent Becoming glabrous.

glabrous Smooth, bald.

gleocystidia A type of pleurocystidia which is highly refractive in tissue that has been revived in potassium hydroxide. Synonomous with chrysocystidia.

glutinous Having a highly viscous gelatinous layer, an exteme condition of viscidity.

gregarious Growing in numerous to dense groups but not clustered as in 'cespitose'.

group All the related varieties of one species.

habit The way in which mushrooms are found growing, i.e., whether singly to numerous to cespitose, and the aspect of their forms.

habitat The substrate in which the mushrooms are found.

hemispheric (of the cap) Resembling a hemisphere. See Diagram A.

heteromorphic (of the gill) Used to describe the type of gill edge which is composed of microscopic cell types different from that on the gill surface or face.

homomorphic (of the gill) Used to describe the type of gill edge which is composed of cell types similar to that on the gill surface or face.

humicolous Growing in humus.

hygrophanous Markedly fading in color when drying.

hymenium The layer of fertile spore-bearing cells on the gill. See Appendix 1.

hypha, hyphae Individual cells of the mycelium.

incurved (of the margin) Curved inwards.

indigenous Native to a certain region.

KOH Potassium hydroxide, an agent commonly used to revive dried mushroom material for microscopic study at a concentration of 2½% (2½ grams of KOH in 97½ grams of distilled water).

lamellae Gills.

lamellulae Short intermediate gills not extending the entire distance from the cap margin to the gill attachment.

lignicolous Growing in wood or on a substratum composed of decayed wood.

lignin The basic organic substance of woody tissue other than cellulose.

lubricous Slightly slippery but not viscid.

macroscopic Visible to the naked eye.

meiosis The process of reduction division by which a single cell with one nucleus divides into four cells with one nucleus apiece. Each nucleus has one half the genetic material of the parent cell.

membranous Thin, tissue-like, as in a homogeneous membrane.

micron (μ) One millionth of a meter, 10^{-9} meters, one thousandth of a millimeter.

microscopic Visible only with the aid of a microscope.

mitosis The process of nuclear division in a cell by which the chromosomes are replicated and divided equally to two 'daughter' nuclei.

mononucleate The condition where a cell has only one nucleus.

mottled Spotted, as from the uneven ripening of the spores in the genus *Panaeolus*.

mycology The study of fungi.

mycophagist A person (or animal) that eats fungi.

mycorrhizal A peculiar type of symbiotic relationship a mushroom mycelium may form with the roots of a seed plant.

naematolomoid (of cystidia) Having the kind of sterile cells on the gill surface which are especially characteristic of the genus *Naematoloma*. See chrysocystidia.
(of mushrooms) Resembling species of *Naematoloma*.

nanometer 10^{-7} meters, $\frac{1}{10}$ of a micron, one ten thousandth of a millimeter.

nomenclature Any system of classification.

nucleate Having nuclei.

nucleus, nuclei A concentrated mass of differentiated protoplasm in all cells which plays an integral role in the reproduction and continuation of genetic information to 'daughter' cells.

obtuse Blunt as opposed to pointed.

ochraceous Light orangish brown to pale yellow-brown.

olivaceous Olive gray-brown.

ovoid Oval to egg shaped.

pallid Very pale in color, almost a dull whitish.

partial veil The inner veil of tissue extending from the cap margin to the stem and at first covering the gills. See Diagram C.

pellicle A skin-like covering on the cap, often gelatinous and separable.

persistent Not deteriorating with age; present throughout the life of the fruiting body.

phototropic Sensitive to light.

pileus The cap of the mushroom.

pileocystidia Sterile cells on the surface of the cap.

pith The central stuffing of stems of some mushrooms.

pleurocystidia Sterile cells on the surface of the gills; sometimes called 'facial cystidia'.

pliant Flexible.

pore A circular depression evident on the end of spores in many species.

pruinose Having the appearance of being powdered due to an abundance of caulocystidia on the stem surface.

pseudorhiza A long root-like extension of the stem.

psilocybian Belonging to the psilocybin-containing mushroom complex; not necessarily of the genus *Psilocybe*.
latently psilocybian Some collections contain psilocybin.

psilocyboid Resembling species of *Psilocybe* in general appearance.

radicate With a pseudorhiza, tapering downwards into a narrow root.

reticulate (of the cap) Marked by lines.

rhizomorphs Cord-like strands of twisted hyphae present around the base of the stem.

rimose (of the cap) Cracked.

rudimentary Primitive, undeveloped.

scanning electron microscope An electronic microscope which scans an object in a vacuum with a beam of electrons resulting in an image of high resolution that is displayed through a television monitor.

seceding (of the gills) Used to describe the condition where the gills have separated in their attachment to the stem and have the appearance of being free. Often leaving longitudinal lines on the stem where the gills once were connected. See Diagram B.

shamanic A term used to describe any religion which embraces the belief that only special persons or priests are capable of influencing the spirits or the supernatural.

sinuate (of the gills) The kind of attachment which seems to be notched before reaching the stem. See Diagram B.

sordid Dingy-looking.

spores The reproductive cells or 'seeds' of fungi borne on specialized cells.

sporocarps Any mushroom having spores.

squamulose Covered with small scales.

sterigmata Elongated appendages or 'arms'

on the basidium upon which spores are borne. See Appendix 1.

stipe   Stem of a mushroom.

Strophariaceae   The family of mushroom containing the closely allied genera *Naematoloma, Psilocybe,* and *Stropharia.*

stropharioid   Resembling species of *Stropharia,* having a membranous ring, a convex cap, and purplish brown spores.

subclose   In reference to the spacing of the gills, between close and crowded. See Diagram C.

subdistant   In reference to the spacing of the gills, between close and distant. See Diagram C.

subequal (of the stem)   Not quite equal.

substratum   The substance in which mushrooms grow.

superior   A term used to designate the location of the annulus in the upper one third of the stem.

tawny   Approximately the color of a lion.

terrestrial   Growing on the ground.

trama   The fleshy part of the cap beneath the cap cuticle and fertile spore-bearing layer of the gill.

translucent   Transmitting light diffusely, semi-transparent.

umbilicate (of the cap)   Depressed in the center. See Diagram A.

umbo   A knob-like protrusion in the center of the cap.

umbonate   Having an umbo. See Diagram A.

uncinate   A type of gill attachment. See Diagram B.

undulating   Wavy.

universal veil   An outer layer of tissue enveloping the cap and stem of some mushrooms, best seen in the youngest stages of development.

variety   A sub-species epithet used to describe a consistently appearing variation of a particular mushroom species.

veil   A tissue covering the mushrooms as they develop. See definitions of partial veil and universal veil, and Diagram C.

viscid   Slimy, slippery, or sticky to the touch. Enhanced in moist conditions.

zonate   Having a band-like zone.

BIBLIOGRAPHIES

Annotated Bibliography of General Mushroom Field Guides

There are three books especially recommended for their information as general mushroom field guides and as simplified manuals for microscopy techniques and chemical reagents: Lange and Hora's *Collins Guide to Mushrooms and Toadstools* (New York: E.P. Dutton & Co., 1963), Alexander Smith's *Mushrooms in Their Natural Habitat* (New York: Hafner Press, 1949), and Orson K. Miller's *Mushrooms of North America* (New York: E.P. Dutton & Co., 1972; paperback 1977). A recently published book dealing in depth with microscopy techniques is *How to Identify Mushrooms III: Microscopic Features* (Eureka, Calif.: Mad River Press, 1977) by D. Largent, D. Johnson, and R. Watling.

Bandoni, R.J., and Szczawinski, A.F. 1976. *Guide to Common Mushrooms of British Columbia.* Victoria, B.C.: British Columbia Provincial Museum. An excellent general field guide.

Kauffman, C.H. 1918. *The Gilled Mushrooms of Michigan and the Great Lakes Region.* Vol. I and II. Reprint. New York: Dover Publications, 1976. Though these books were written years ago, they contain much useful information. The keys to species are fairly good, though many names have since been changed.

Kreiger, L.C. 1936. *The Mushroom Handbook.* Reprint. New York: Dover Publications, 1967. Somewhat interesting to browse through though not very practical as a field guide. Outdated.

Lange, M., and Hora, F.B. 1963. *Collins Guide to Mushrooms and Toadstools.* New York: E.P. Dutton & Co. Though this book was originally oriented to be a field guide for

European mushrooms, many of the North American species are covered. It is simply laid out with beautiful watercolors. Highly recommended, especially for beginners.

Largent, D.L. 1977. *How to Identify Mushrooms (to Genus) Using Only Macroscopic Features.* Rev. ed. Eureka, Calif.: Mad River Press. This book places special emphasis on explanation of mycological terms and illustration of mushroom morphology. The drawings are superb and the book modestly priced. Does not contain any photographs. An excellent addition to one's mushroom book collection.

McIlvaine, C. 1900. *One Thousand American Fungi.* Reprint. New York: Dover Publications, 1971. A collector's item in the first edition (Indianapolis: Bowen-Merrill Co.). Very interesting, though antiquated.

McKenny, M., and Stuntz, D.E. 1962. *The Savory Wild Mushroom.* Rev. ed. Seattle: Univ. of Washington Press. A good general mushroom guide to species common to the Pacific Northwest. However, the color is not quite accurate.

Miller, O.K., Jr. 1972. *Mushrooms of North America.* New York: E.P. Dutton & Co.; paperback 1977. Though containing some inaccuracies, especially in relation to psilocybes and panaeoli, this is one of the best mushroom books on the market. The color plates are superior. Expensive but well worth it.

Rinaldi, A., and Tynaldo, V. 1972. *The Complete Book of Mushrooms.* New York: Crown Publishers. Has nice watercolors. An intriguing book but not one which I would recommend to the low-budget amateur.

Smith, A.H. 1949. *Mushrooms in Their Natural Habitats.* New York: Hafner Press. An excellent resource for students of gilled mushroom mycology. Complete with extensive macroscopic and microscopic features for the species covered. Comes with 3-D Sawyer slides. Highly recommended.

———. 1969. *The Mushroom Hunter's Field Guide.* Rev. and enlarged. Ann Arbor: Univ. of Michigan Press. Excellent in combination with Smith, 1975.

———. 1975. *A Field Guide to Western Mushrooms.* Ann Arbor: Univ. of Michigan Press. This book shows some of the more unusual species of the west not in the companion volume. Both of these are highly recommended.

General Bibliography

Alexopolous, C.H. 1970. *Introductory to Mycology.* New York: John Wiley and Sons.

Bennedict, R.G., Brady, L.R., Smith, A.H., and Tyler, V.E. 1962. "Occurence of Psilocybin and Psilocin in Certain *Conocybe* and *Psilocybe* Species." *Lloydia* 25:156-159.

Bennedict, R.G., Tyler, V.E., and Watling, R. 1967. "Blueing in *Conocybe, Psilocybe,* and *Stropharia* Species and the Detection of Psilocybin." *Lloydia 30: 150–175.*

Brady, L.R., Bennedict, R.G., Tyler, V.E., Stuntz, D.E., Malone, M.H. 1975. "Identification of *Conocybe filaris* as a Toxic Basidiomycete." *Lloydia* 38:172–173.

Chilton, W.S., and Ott, J. 1976. "Toxic Metabolites of *Amanita pantherina, A. cothurnata, A. muscaria,* and other Amanita species." *Lloydia* 39:150–157.

Cooke, M.C. 1883. *Handbook of British Fungi.* 2nd ed. London.

Dennis, R.W.G., Orton, P.D., and Hora, F.B. 1960. "New Checklist of British Agarics and Boleti." T.B.M.S. Supp. 43, June.

Earle, F.S. 1906. "Algunos (hongos) Cubanos." Inf. An. Estae. *Agron Cuba* 1:225–242.

Enos, L. 1970. *A Key to the American Psilocybin Mushroom.* Lemon Grove, Calif.: Youniverse Press

Furst, P.T. 1972. *Flesh of the Gods.* New York: Praeger Publishers.

Guzmán, G., and Pérez, Patraca, A.M. 1972. "Las Especies Conocidas Del Genero *Panaeolus* En Mexico." *Boletin de la Sociedad Mexicana de Micologia*, no. 6.

Guzmán, G. 1976. "Description and Chemical Analysis of a New Species of Halucinogenic *Psilocybe* from the Pacific Northwest." *Mycologia* 68:1261–1267.

———, Ott, J., and Pollock, S.H. 1976. "Psychotropic Mycoflora of Washington, Idaho, Oregon, California, and British Colombia." *Mycologia* 68:1267–1272.

———, 1976–1977. Personal communications.

Heim, R., Wasson, R.G., and collaborators. 1958. *Les Champignons Hallucinogènes du Mexique.* Vol. 6. Paris: Editions du Museum National d'Histoire Naturelle.

Heim, R. 1963. *Les Champignons Toxiques et Hallucinogènes.* Paris, N. Boubee.

Heim, R., Hofman, A., and Tscherter, H. 1966. "Sur une Intoxication Collective a Syndrome Psilocybien Causée en France par un *Copelandia." Comptes Rendus Hebdomadaire des Seances de l'Academie des Sciences Series D* 262:509–523.

Heim, R. (with Cailleux, R., Wasson, R.G., and Thevenard, P.) 1967. "Nouvelles Investigations sur Les Champignons Hallucinogènes." Paris: Editions du Museum National D'Histoire Naturelle.

Heim, R. 1971. "A Propos des Propriétés Hallucinogènes du *Psilocybe semilanceata." Le Naturaliste Canadien* 98:415–424.

Hofmann, A., Heim, R., and Tscherter, H. 1963. "Présence de la Psilocybine dans une Espéce Europeen d'Agaric, le *Psilocybe semilanceata* (Fr.)." *Comptes Rendus Hebdomadaire des Seances de l'Academie des Seances.*

Kauffman, C.H. 1971. *The Gilled Mushrooms of Michigan and the Great Lakes Region.* Vol. I and II. New York: Dover Publications.

Lange, J.E. 1923. "Studies in the Agarics of Denmark. Part 5: Ecological Notes. The Hygrophorei. *Stropharia* and *Hypholoma.* Supplementary Notes to Parts I–III." *Dansk Bot. Ark.* Vol. IV, no. 4 pp. 1–55.

Miller, O.K., Jr. 1968. "Fungi of the Yukon and Alaska." *Mycologia* 60:1201–1203.

———— and Farr, David F., 1975. *An Index of the Common Fungi of North America (Synonymy and Common Names)*. Germany: J. Cramer.

Miller, O.K., Jr. 1976. Personal communication.

Murrill, W.A. 1916. "A Very Dangerous Mushroom, *Panaeolus venenosus* sp. nov." *Mycologia* 8:186–187.

————. 1922. "Dark Spored Agarics I. *Drosophila, Hypholoma,* and *Pilosace.*" *Mycologia* 14:61–76.

————. 1922. "Dark Spored Agarics II. *Gomphidius* and *Stropharia.*" *Mycologia* 14:121–142.

————. W.A. 1923. "Dark Spored Agarics V. *Psilocybe.*" *Mycologia* 15:1–55.

Ola'h, G.M. 1969. "A Taxonomical and Physiological Study of the Genus *Panaeolus* with Latin Descriptions of the New Species." *Revue de Mycologie*, vol. 33, no. 4, pp. 284–290.

————. 1969. "Le Genre *Panaeolus:* Essai Taxonomique et Physiologique." *Revue de Mycologie*, Memoire Hors-Serie 10.

————. 1967. "Nouvelle Espéce de la Flore Mycologique Canadienne." *Naturaliste Canadien* 94:573–587.

————. 1973. "The Fine Structure of *Psilocybe quebecensis.*" *Mycopathologia et Mycologia applicata*, Vol. 49, no. 4, pp. 321–338.

Peck, C.H. 1897. *Annual Report of the State Botanist of the State of New York*. Albany: James B. Lyon.

Pollock, S.H. 1975. "The Psilocybin Mushroom Pandemic." *Journal of Psychedelic Drugs,* vol. 7, no. 1, pp. 73–84.

————. 1976. "Psilocybian Mycetismus with Special Reference to *Panaeolus,*" Journal of Psychedelic Drugs, vol. 8, no. 1, pp. 45–56.

Puget Sound Mycological Society. 1972. "Mushroom Poisoning in the Pacific Northwest." Seattle.

Repke, D.B., and Leslie, D.T. 1976. Personal communication.

Robbers, J.E., Tyler, V.E., and Ola'h, G.M. 1969. "Additional Evidence Supporting the Occurrence of Psilocybin in *Panaeolus foenisecii.*" *Lloydia* 32:399–400.

Sahagun, F.B. *The Florentine Codex, General History of the Things of New Spain.* Santa Fe: Author J. Anderson and Charles E. Dibble, The School of American Research and the University of Utah.

Singer, R., and Smith, A.H. 1958. "New Species of *Psilocybe.*" *Mycologia* 50:141–142.

————. 1958. "Mycological Investigations on *Teonanácatl,* The Mexican Hallucinogenic Mushroom. Part I: The History of *Teonanácatl,* Field Work and Culture Work. Part II: A Taxonomic Monograph of *Psilocybe,* Section Caerulescentes." *Mycologia* 50: 239–303.

Singer, R. 1975. *The Agaricales in Modern Taxonomy*. 3rd ed. J. Cramer Co.

Smith, A.H. 1946. "New and Unusual Dark Spored Agarics from North America," *Journal of the Mitchell Society*, 4:195–200.

————. 1948. "Studies on Dark-Spored Agarics." *Mycologia* 40:669–707.

————. 1949. *Mushrooms in Their Natural Habitats*. New York: Hafner Press.

————. 1951. "North American Species of *Naematoloma*." *Mycologia* 43:468–515.

————, and Singer, R. 1964. *A Monograph on the Genus Galerina Earle*. Portland: Sawyer's.

Snell, W.H., Dick, E.A. 1971. *A Glossary of Mycology*. Cambridge: Harvard Univ. Press.

Stuntz, D.E. 1976. Personal communication.

Wasson, V.P. and R.G. 1957. *Mushrooms, Russia, and History*. New York: Pantheon Books.

Wasson, R.G. 1958. "The Divine Mushroom: Primitive Religion and Hallucinatory Agents." *Proceedings of the American Philosophical Society*. 102:221–223.

————, and Heim, R. 1959. "The Hallucinogenic Mushrooms of Mexico: An Adventure in Ethnomycological Exploration." *Transcripts of the New York Academy of Sciences*. 21:325–339.

Wasson, R.G. 1961. "The Hallucinogenic Fungi of Mexico: An Inquiry into the Origin of the Religious Idea Among Primitive Peoples." *Harvard Univ. Botanical Museum Leaflets*, 19:147.

————. 1972. *Soma, Divine Mushroom of Immortality*. New York: Harcourt, Brace, Jovanovich.

Watling, R. 1977. Personal communication.

Vergeer, P. Personal communication.

ACKNOWLEDGEMENTS

WITHOUT the unwavering support of Dr. Michael Beug and Catherine Scates, this book would not have been possible. They have my most sincere and heartfelt thanks.

Dr. Gastón Guzmán and Dr. Roy Watling have been very helpful in clearing up some of the difficulties and ambiguities I encountered in this area of fungal taxonomy. The time they spent reviewing and criticizing my keys is very much appreciated.

Dr. Daniel Stuntz and Paul Vergeer were helpful in finding reference material, often buried in remote niches of mycological literature. I am very grateful for the time they spent researching some of the more obscure references.

Steven Schnoor and Ann Lasko did an excellent job illustrating the diagrams. I thank them for their time and energy.

Jeremy Bigwood's general assistance and the use of his beautiful field photographs are appreciated.

Roger Golub first introduced me to scanning electron microscopy. I have many enjoyable memories of the marathon sessions we spent in front of the SEM. Thanks also to James Sheets, Marty Beagle, and Dr. Donald Humphreys for their general support in SEM-related studies. (All micrographs were produced on a Coates and Welter Model 100 Scanning Electron Microscope at Evergreen State College).

As for fellow mushroom hunters, I have enjoyed the times spent in the field and on the road with Steven Pollock, Gary Menser, Dale Leslie, Dave Cotton, Fritz Johnson, Pam Lewis, and John Stamets.

Bob Harris has always encouraged my work. His dedication to producing a good field guide has been a welcome addition to the Homestead Book Company's desire to publish this book. I have well enjoyed the times spent hunting mushrooms with both Bob Harris and David Tatelman.

Last but not least, a special thanks to the people at Evergreen State College, especially Patricia May, whose patience and support during the creation of this book is very much appreciated.

ILLUSTRATION CREDITS

Photographs

Dr. Michael Beug
FIGS. 3, 9, 32, 34, 37, 46

Jeremy Bigwood
FIGS. 11, 13, 18, 24, 27, 29, 43, 54, 62

Bob Harris
COVER, FIGS. 1, 2, 4, 15, 40, 48, 50, 51, 52, 53, 55, 56, 59, 60

Jim Jacobs
FIG. 44

Gary Menser
FIG. 26

Steven Pollock
FIG. 16

Kit Scates
FIGS. 5, 7, 8, 10, 14, 17, 20, 21, 22, 25, 31, 33, 35, 38, 39, 45, 47, 49

Paul Stamets
FIGS. 6, 12, 19, 23, 28, 30, 41, 42, 57, 58, 61, 63–75

Ben Woo
FIG. 36

Diagrams

Steven Schnoor
DIAGRAMS A, B, C, D

Ann Lasko
DIAGRAM E